"Richard Rice brings together two things often separated: philosophical and theological explanations for suffering, and the practical struggle of persons trying to make sense of suffering in their own lives or the lives of others close to them. He surveys seven widely embraced approaches and concludes with a thoughtful chapter that provides guidance on developing one's personal response to suffering. An open theist himself, Rice is remarkably even-handed in describing how each of the approaches offers comfort as well as puzzles and unanswered questions. This book provides a rich resource both for those trying to understand their own suffering and for those who work with them and minister to them."

William Hasker, Huntington University

"Writing on the problem of suffering, Richard Rice combines a philosopher's keen intellect with a pastoral heart to produce an incisive and helpful book. The work is clear, down to earth, and useful for those who suffer or are troubled by the fact of suffering in our world. The many illustrations from real life are illuminating, and the discussions of the various approaches to evil are fair and sensible. I recommend the book highly."

Stephen T. Davis, Claremont McKenna College

"Questions about suffering never go away, nor do our attempts to explain it and live courageously in spite of it. Among the myriad of books on the topic, Richard Rice's is distinguished by its union of theoretical and personal concerns—by the way it brings together the concrete experience of suffering and the different ways careful thinkers have tried to explain its presence in the world. Accessible and practical, as well as philosophically informed, *Suffering and the Search for Meaning* will be of great value to physicians and other care providers as they seek to understand and respond to the full range of their clients' needs."

Harold G. Koenig, MD, professor of psychiatry and director of the Center for Spirituality, Theology and Health, Duke University Medical Center

"Pain and suffering are integral to human life, but never easy to understand or to deal with. Richard Rice's *Suffering and the Search for Meaning* brings a new dimension to reflection on the meaning of suffering, one deeply imbued with the best theological and philosophical thinking, but also attuned to contemporary human experience. After a clear analysis of the advantages and drawbacks of six classic options, he argues for a practical theodicy that does not try to make final sense of suffering but that helps those in the midst of suffering to respond in a resourceful way that will enhance the meaning of life."
Bernard McGinn, University of Chicago Divinity School

"Those who suffer know two things: that suffering calls for silence and that, eventually, it seeks to be understood. Richard Rice respects this double knowledge, honors the limits of what we can say in a crisis and humbly surveys a range of responses to suffering to help his readers speak faithfully in and of pain—their own, and others."
Matt Jenson, Biola University

"*Suffering and the Search for Meaning* is a beautiful book. Richard Rice writes gracefully, gently, wisely and sensitively about this most troubling and persistent problem—the pain and suffering of our lives and the lives of those we love. Rice provides a careful and accessible engagement with the most enduring 'solutions' that theologians and philosophers have offered to this problem. He is always careful to give each one its best hearing but never shies away from probing the weaknesses of a particular theodicy. He draws effortlessly and poignantly from popular culture, literature and yesterday's headlines to provide lively illustrations of his ideas. To read this book is to be guided gently, and to be addressed with respect and dignity, by one of the truly gifted pastoral theologians of our day."
Michael Lodahl, Point Loma Nazarene University

SUFFERING
and the Search
for Meaning

Contemporary Responses to the Problem of Pain

RICHARD RICE

IVP Academic

An imprint of InterVarsity Press
Downers Grove, Illinois

InterVarsity Press
P.O. Box 1400, Downers Grove, IL 60515-1426
ivpress.com
email@ivpress.com

InterVarsity Press® is the book-publishing division of InterVarsity Christian Fellowship/USA®, a movement of students and faculty active on campus at hundreds of universities, colleges and schools of nursing in the United States of America, and a member movement of the International Fellowship of Evangelical Students. For information about local and regional activities, visit intervarsity.org.

Cover design: Cindy Kiple
Interior design: Beth McGill
Images: CSA Images/Color Pintstock Collection Getty Images

ISBN 978-0-8308-4037-3 (print)
ISBN 978-0-8308-8020-1 (digital)

Printed in the United States of America ∞

InterVarsity Press is committed to ecological stewardship and to the conservation of natural resources in all our operations. This book was printed using sustainably sourced paper.

Library of Congress Cataloging-in-Publication Data
Rice, Richard, 1944-
  Suffering and the search for meaning : contemporary responses to the
  problem of pain / Richard Rice.
      pages cm
  Includes bibliographical references and indexes.
  ISBN 978-0-8308-4037-3 (pbk. : alk. paper)
  1. Suffering—Religious aspects—Christianity. 2. Theodicy. I. Title.
  BT732.7.R525 2014
  231'.8—dc23
                                                                      2014011886

| P | 20 | 19 | 18 | 17 | 16 | 15 | 14 | 13 | 12 | 11 | 10 | 9 | 8 | 7 | 6 | 5 | 4 | 3 | 2 |
| Y | 33 | 32 | 31 | 30 | 29 | 28 | 27 | 26 | 25 | 24 | 23 | 22 | 21 | 20 | 19 | 18 | 17 |

For Rosa, Alexa, Taylor and Lachlan

CONTENTS

PREFACE

AFTER TEACHING VARIOUS RELIGION CLASSES at a liberal arts campus for many years, I was asked to provide a graduate course at a neighboring health sciences university on the subject of suffering. The students came from a number of professional programs and represented different stages of their training. I wasn't sure how interested people heading for careers in fields such as dentistry, medicine, nursing, physical therapy and public health would be in a course that had a heavy philosophical component. After all, the problem of evil has occupied great minds for centuries, and since my academic background lies in philosophical theology, I felt a responsibility to expose the students to some serious discussions of the topic.

What happened as the course progressed was a revelation of sorts. Far from turning the students off, the various responses to suffering we examined generated animated discussions. The students seriously probed the logic of these positions and then they raised more urgent concerns. How did the views we were examining relate to the concrete evil, the personal suffering, they encountered in their professional lives? How should they respond to the suffering of people in their care? What answers could they give when someone asked them *why? Why is this happening to me or to someone I love?*

There was clearly a connection between the philosophical question of evil and the practical, personal challenge of concrete human suffering. Serious reflections on the problem of evil ultimately touched on pressing personal needs, and pressing personal concerns gave rise to serious intellectual discussions. I came to realize that the experience of suffering provides a "fast track" to virtually all the fundamental philosophical and theological issues that had interested me over the years, such as creation—*what kind of world did God create? And what kind of God created the world?*— and providence—*what is God doing in the world? And what in the world is God doing?*

This book is driven by one central question: How can ideas about suffering help those who face the experience of suffering? People respond to life's great losses in a variety of ways. Each of these explanations has attractive features, yet each one leaves lingering questions. So, in spite of our efforts and our hopes, suffering never makes perfect sense. At the same time, knowing what thoughtful people have to say about suffering can help us understand what suffering people are going through. And there are many elements, or "fragments," in their interpretations that can help us respond resourcefully to suffering ourselves. So the interface between theories about suffering and the practical challenge of facing suffering deserves careful exploration.

After an introductory chapter, this book examines a spectrum of views, including perfect plan theodicy, the free will defense, soul making theodicy, cosmic conflict theodicy, openness of God theodicy, process theodicy and theodicies of protest. The concluding chapter offers some suggestions for the development of a practical theodicy. Since the specific purpose of this book is to bring together practical and theoretical concerns, each chapter begins with a personal account of someone's response to suffering and proceeds to explore the framework of meaning to which this response points. It is natural for anyone who reflects on these matters to develop a position of his or her own, and I have mine. But although I have participated in the formulation of open theism (as it is generally known) over the past thirty years, the purpose of this discussion is to present a variety of perspectives, not to argue for the superiority of any particular view.

As the students in my class reminded me, the need to make sense of suffering is just as pervasive as suffering itself, so its intellectual challenges are not just for intellectuals. There are people who have neither the background, the time, nor the appetite for technical philosophical discussions, but are nevertheless concerned about the large-scale questions that theodicies deal with. This book is intended for them. It was written with the proverbial "general reader" in mind, that is, a thoughtful person who, while not a specialist in theology or philosophy nor intending to become one, is nevertheless interested in the issues that suffering raises and expects to gain something of personal value from a thoughtful discussion of them. Its goal is to describe the probative value and the personal appeal that various approaches to suffering provide, as well as to note the conceptual and practical limitations of each. I hope that it will serve as an invitation for further reflection and a source of personal encouragement.

Though modest in size, this endeavor has been a long time in the making, and I have incurred a number of intellectual debts along the way, far too many to acknowledge individually. I think first of all of the students in the various classes I have taught on suffering. Like many teachers, I am sure I learned more from them than they ever learned from me. I have also benefited from the collaboration of admirable colleagues in the schools of religion at two universities—Loma Linda University and La Sierra University. A few

whose perspectives on the theology of suffering have been particularly helpful to me in shaping my own are Wilber Alexander, Ivan
Blazen, Fritz Guy, David R. Larson and Sigve Tonstad.

I am also deeply grateful to those who shared with me insights
from their personal losses. They include Donna Carlson, Bailey
and Judy Gillespie, James Harris, Jack and Marlys Jacobson, Iris
Landa, Kay Nelson, Don and Gladys Schlinkert, and David and
Janet Wilkins.

I am indebted to two editors at InterVarsity Press. Gary Deddo
was the first to assist me in developing this project, and the counsel
and encouragement of David Congdon have been immensely
helpful to me in bringing it to a conclusion. I also benefited from
the careful reading of two anonymous reviewers. Their comments
and suggestions led to a number of revisions and improvements.

Last, and most important, my family has contributed to these
reflections in ways that surpass description. As always my wife,
Gail, has been a wellspring of love and good humor. During the
past few years we have shared the pain of losing three of our parents
and the joy of welcoming four grandchildren into the world. Our
daughter Alison and her husband, Olivier, have two adorable
daughters. Our son Jonathan and his wife, Rebekah, are the parents
of two energetic boys. I have dedicated this book to these four
young lives, in the hope that their sufferings will be few and the
prayer that they will find in God a very present help in trouble.

1

MY GOD, WHY?

The Question That Never Goes Away

A CALL TO THINK SERIOUSLY ABOUT SUFFERING

One evening soon after I started teaching college, there was a knock at our front door. It was a student in one of my religion classes. She was visibly upset. "Your mother's been in an accident and she needs you," she blurted out.

"Where is she?" I asked.

"It happened just down the street."

Mother was visiting us from across the country at the time. She had accepted an invitation to go to a prayer meeting several miles away with two friends. On the way home, Mom was sitting in the back seat on the passenger side. Her ride dropped off the lady in the front seat first, and since they were only five minutes or so from our house, Mom stayed where she was—a decision that probably saved her life. They made a left turn onto our street and before they cleared the intersection, a speeding car from down the road crashed into them. The right side of the car took the full force of the collision.

My wife and I rushed to the scene. Mother was already in the ambulance, conscious but in severe pain, and we headed for the nearest hospital. We searched for reassuring things to say. "Everything will be all right. We'll get you the best doctor we can. You know Jesus loves you." "I know he does," she said. As things turned out, her right hip was broken. But she had an excellent surgeon and made a full recovery.

Everyone has stories like this to tell. And our family has others as well. Sooner or later we or someone close to us meets with illness, accident or worse. Suffering is universal and no one is immune.

Contrasting Approaches to Suffering

There are hundreds of books on suffering. A bookstore of any size has stacks of them. Some are "survival" stories, moving accounts by or about people who have gone through a tragedy or lost someone dear to them, like the grief memoirs whose numbers have grown in the past few years. Others are "how-to" books, with lists of things you need to do in order to "cope," "move on" or "reach closure" when you find yourself in a painful situation.

In the same store you will also find books on the topic of evil. I don't mean dark dramas about monsters, demons or aliens. I mean serious discussions about the nature of the world we live in. For centuries suffering has driven people to ask questions about God. If God is perfectly good and powerful, the argument goes, then evil is incomprehensible. After all, a good God would want to eliminate it, and an all-powerful God would be able to. So why does evil exist? Why do people suffer? What possible explanation can it have?

The difference between these various approaches is rather sharp. Books of the first and second sort sit in the self-help or popular psychology section of the store. The others rest among weighty tomes on theology or philosophy. The division isn't airtight, of course. Philosophers occasionally touch on the practical conse-quences of their theories, and how-to books sometimes appeal to philosophical positions. But ordinarily a book will focus on one concern rather than the other.

Our goal in the following pages is to bring these various concerns together—to explore the connection between ideas *about* suffering and the personal experience *of* suffering. Since suffering comes to everyone, philosophers included, over the long run we need an approach to suffering that is more than just a philosophical treatise on the subject or a how-to book for sufferers or caregivers. We need something that probes the connection between these concerns—the relation between theological convictions and practical experience.

We need an approach like this because ideas have consequences, as it is often said, and in the case of suffering these consequences can be tremendous. In fact, there may be no experience in life where ideas play a more important role. As Wendy Farley observes, "The way we interpret suffering has a great deal to do with how we experience suffering."[1] And the way people respond to crisis often reflects their particular vision of how, when and why God acts or doesn't act in the world. When we consider various responses to suffering, therefore, it is important for us to explore the relation of each religious or philosophical interpretation to concrete, lived experience. Because suffering is such a formidable and complex challenge, we need all the resources we have to meet it.

Of course, though closely connected, theory and experience are seldom in perfect alignment. When sufferers view a great loss through the lens of their religious convictions, they are sometimes reassured, sometimes perplexed, sometimes disillusioned. Once in a while, people find that their suffering fits comfortably, and comfortingly, within a familiar framework of beliefs. Their long-held

---

[1]Wendy Farley, "The Practice of Theodicy," in *Pain Seeking Understanding: Suffering, Medicine, and Faith*, ed. Margaret E. Mohrmann and Mark J. Hanson (Cleveland, OH: Pilgrim, 1999), p. 103.

ideas and convictions give them great peace. Quite often, however, suffering forces people to change their views about God—sometimes dramatically. "Given what I believe about God," one may say, "my suffering makes perfect sense. I know exactly what it means." "Given what I have always thought," another may say, "my suffering makes no sense at all. Now I don't know what to believe." So there are people whose suffering draws them closer to God, and others whose suffering drives them away.

Some of the most influential discussions of suffering come from those whose suffering raises serious questions. "There is one question that matters, and only one," says Harold Kushner in his bestselling book on suffering. "Why do bad things happen to good people? All other theological conversation is intellectually diverting."[2] Kushner emphasizes what everyone knows. Suffering can be a great obstacle to faith. When people don't believe in God, more often than not, the number one reason they give is the suffering they have experienced or the suffering they see in the world around them. And for people who do believe, suffering is still a tremendous challenge. As philosopher Alvin Plantinga sees it, the argument from evil is the one argument against God's existence worth taking seriously.[3]

SUFFERING AS LIFE-CHANGING LOSS

People use the word "suffering" to refer to a great many things, from minor inconveniences to much more serious matters. But the sort of suffering we are talking about isn't something that merely interrupts or complicates our lives. It isn't something we can make

---

[2]Harold S. Kushner, *When Bad Things Happen to Good People* (New York: Schocken Books, 1981), p. 6.
[3]Alvin Plantinga, "A Christian Life Partly Lived," in *Philosophers Who Believe: The Spiritual Journeys of Eleven Leading Thinkers,* ed. Kelly James Clark (Downers Grove, IL: InterVarsity Press, 1993), pp. 72-73.

a few adjustments to accommodate and get on with business as usual. The sort of suffering that concerns us here is like a natural disaster. It sweeps away all the familiar landmarks—just like the tidal waves that devastated southern Asia in late 2004 and the eastern coast of Japan in early 2011, or the hurricanes that inundated New Orleans and battered the shores of New Jersey and New York, or the devastating floods of 2010 in Brazil and Australia, or the rash of tornadoes that recently crossed the midsection of the United States. Sometimes suffering engulfs large numbers of people, and sometimes it cuts into the lives of a few. Either way, great suffering is like a tsunami or Katrina of the soul—it alters the landscape of our lives. It transports us to a strange new world. And everything about us changes . . . permanently. Suffering, to put it simply, is life-changing loss.

In a horrific accident college professor Jerry Sittser lost his mother, his wife and one of his three children. A drunk driver crashed into the van he was driving. When he climbed out of the wreck and saw the effects of the collision, a powerful sensation settled over him. He began to realize that things would never be the same. By the time the ambulance reached the hospital, two hours later, he knew he could never go back to the life he had before. In his words, he "stepped out into a whole new world."[4]

When someone suffers, she loses an essential part of herself, something central to the meaning and purpose of her life. What is lost may be a physical ability, someone or something we love, a career, or an income. A serious illness or injury can leave self-sufficient people dependent on others—changing their lives forever along with their families' lives. Losing a loved one can leave someone feeling that the best part of her life is over, and nothing

---

[4]Jerry Sittser, *A Grace Disguised: How the Soul Grows Through Loss* (Grand Rapids: Zondervan, 1996), p. 21.

will fill the emptiness that lies ahead. Losing a job in our success-oriented culture can have devastating effects. Take away someone's ability to "contribute to society," and he easily wonders if his life has any value. People also suffer when they see their dreams evaporate. Suffering can destroy things that took years to accomplish or accumulate. It can obliterate the work of a lifetime. When retirement accounts plummet and homes go into foreclosure, as they did during the economic crisis several years ago, many people feel that they have lost their future. Their sense of security vanishes.

Suffering dashes hopes and shatters dreams, and when it does, it makes us strangers to ourselves. Sittser is right. To suffer is to enter a world we've never known before. Suffering leaves us feeling isolated, abandoned and betrayed. To use a biblical expression, we feel "the mountains shake in the heart of the sea" (Ps 46:2). We find our world disintegrating.

Suffering can disturb us even when we are not the ones suffering, because suffering anywhere reminds us that suffering is everywhere. I've taught classes on suffering for many years, but I've never kept a file on the topic. I don't need one. All I have to do is check the morning news. It always contains plenty of examples. In fact, by my rough count, ninety percent of the items on a typical front page of the *Los Angeles Times* connect in one way or another to some form of suffering. Whether it's in a far-off corner of the world or just down the street, suffering is everywhere.

Most of us can list disasters that have befallen people we know. Just recalling some of the people I went to school with years ago brings to mind a catalog of tragedies. One died when his motorcycle ran into a truck. Another perished in a traffic accident on her way to meet her husband at the airport. A third died from burns after a space heater set fire to some cleaning fluid. A fourth ended her own life during the holidays one year. A fifth succumbed to breast cancer.

Another has a son who was sentenced to life in prison for killing a fellow high school student when a drug deal went bad. I could go on. So could anyone. We all know people who have suffered greatly.

Suffering and the Meaning of Life

But if suffering is so common, you have to wonder, why do we hear so much about it? Why does something so pervasive upset us? If suffering is just a part of life, why don't we simply accept it and move on? People obviously take great interest in suffering—"If it bleeds, it leads," say newspaper editors—but why? What accounts for its "shock value"? Why do we react with a shudder?

Here's the reason: Suffering unsettles us because it threatens one of our deepest convictions. Whether we are consciously aware of it or not, we all cling to the belief that the world is orderly and life makes sense. This is one of those "basic beliefs" that provide a foundation for everything else we believe . . . and for everything we do, for that matter. It is a part of what we might call a basic existential faith, "our basic confidence in the abiding worth of our lives," as one thinker puts it.[5] Because suffering threatens this visceral confidence that reality is stable and our lives have purpose, we are compelled to make some sense of it. We are driven to look for ways to fit suffering within some framework or structure of meaning. Just as nature abhors a vacuum, our minds abhor absurdity. We need suffering to be sensible.

In fact, this urge to make sense of suffering is just as pervasive as suffering itself. As the ambulance made its way to the hospital after her accident, my mother said, "It happened for a purpose." Here she was, just minutes after a violent collision, wracked with pain, not knowing the extent of her injuries or how they might

---

[5]Schubert M. Ogden, *The Reality of God and Other Essays* (New York: Harper & Row, 1966), p. 37.

affect her life, yet she considered the eternal questions that suffering brings: "Why?" "Why did this happen?" "Why did this happen to me?" And she voiced an answer. She found comfort in the thought that there was a reason, an explanation, for what she was going through. The crash was not an empty, meaningless, random event. There had to be a purpose behind it.

If suffering is life's greatest challenge, nothing is more important than finding a way to meet it. And that, in a nutshell, is the purpose of this book. What can we do to respond creatively and resourcefully to suffering? How can we resist the threat that suffering poses to the meaning of our lives?

Theodicy and the Search for Meaning

In many discussions of suffering, whether technical or not, there is an unusual expression that often appears, and that is the word *theodicy*. The word originated with a seventeenth-century German thinker, Gottfried Wilhelm Leibniz. Along with science, mathematics and metaphysics, Leibniz took a special interest in the problem of evil. And to give his book on the topic a title, he coined the word *theodicy*, combining the Greek words for "justify" (*dikaioō*) and "God" (*theos*). A theodicy is an attempt to justify, or defend, God in the face of evil. And in spite of its philosophical overtones, it is common for people today to use the word to refer to any thoughtful interpretation of suffering.

As a philosophical exercise, a theodicy serves a minimal purpose. It does not presume to explain why specific instances of suffering occur. Its only goal is to show that the presence of evil in the world is not logically incompatible with God's existence. For most of us, this doesn't accomplish very much, even if it succeeds. People who are actually suffering want a good deal more than this. To rebuild our lives after a devastating loss, we surely need more than a philosophical treatise. At least, that is the conventional wisdom. "Sufferers don't need explanations," we often hear. "What they need is compassion. Instead of burdening them with theories, offer them a listening ear, a sympathetic touch, something in the way of concrete, practical assistance."

Not only do suffering people want more than theories, they may not want theories at all. In fact, instead of relieving suffering, theoretical explanations sometimes make it worse. That was true of history's most famous sufferer. When the biblical figure of Job lost everything—property, children and finally his health—three friends came to visit him. They sat in sympathetic silence for seven days, but when they started to speak, the burden of their mission became clear. One by one they gave Job an explanation for his suffering. "Innocent people don't suffer," they told him in effect. "Guilty people do. Your predicament is not a baffling mystery. It is perfectly understandable. For some reason or other, you have brought this suffering on yourself. You deserve what is happening to you."

With friends like these, we are tempted to ask, who needs enemies? No wonder people say that sufferers need compassion rather than theories. But that is only part of the picture. Certainly, no one in the throes of grief or loss wants to sit through an abstract discourse on the nature of reality. But the fact that people in pain don't want explanations doesn't mean they will never want them. As time goes by, those who have endured a great loss often crave nothing more than some serious reflection on their plight.

We noted that suffering alters the landscape of our lives. Its seismic upheavals leave us bewildered and disoriented. In order to continue life's journey in this strange new world, we must thread our way through enormous obstacles. That's where theodicy, reflecting carefully on the nature of suffering, comes in. A theodicy is a kind of map. Its purpose is to locate our suffering on the landscape of human experience and help us find a way through it.

If you are in the middle of a long trip somewhere and you realize that you are lost, the best thing to do is stop and take your bearings. Once you figure out where you are, you can plan your next move. That's what a theodicy can do. A thoughtful response to suffering can help us determine where we are and decide where we should go. By providing an aerial view of our location, so to speak, it gives us a way to place our suffering within the larger landscape of our lives. It's a little like a diagram with a "You are here" dot on it.

To change the comparison, a theodicy is less like emergency surgery than physical therapy. It may not belong in a first aid kit for sufferers, but it does have a place in long term care. Ordinarily, people numbed by enormous loss are not ready for theorizing. What they need most is a helping hand or a shoulder to cry on. Over the long haul, however, they often need something more—a sense of where they are and a reason to keep going. That's where theodicy can help.

A friend of mine lost his son several years ago when an airliner crashed into the Atlantic Ocean taking the lives of everyone on board. He often talks to groups about the experience and how it has shaped his life. Over time the emphasis in his remarks has shifted. Early on, he described the loss in some detail—what happened to his son and how he and the rest of his family reacted. Then he would add some reflections on what this loss might mean. As time went by, however, my friend came to devote less time to the accident and its immediate aftermath and more to the way his religious perspectives have changed. He now views his loss within a well-developed theological framework.

This progression illustrates something important about suffering. Practical problems often have a theoretical side, and this is never more true than when we suffer. Although suffering often swamps us with tremendous practical problems, the challenges don't stop there. We are creatures of thought as well as action and feeling, and suffering raises unavoidable questions. Because suffering threatens the very meaning of life, an effective response to suffering must help us recover that meaning. And for that, careful thinking is indispensable. As Viktor Frankl discovered in the midst of the Holocaust, someone who has a *why* to live can survive almost any *how*.[6] Without a theoretical element, then, without a theodicy of some sort, no practical response to suffering will be enough.

Our objective in the following pages is to look carefully at a number of different theodicies, or thoughtful responses to suffering. As we shall see, each one of them has both a theoretical and a practical side. Each offers an interpretation of suffering and implies that we should adopt certain attitudes and practices in response to it. It is important for us to examine both sides—both the thinking behind the position and its practical applications. Different theories of suffering have different practical consequences and, predictably, different people find certain theodicies more helpful than others. In fact, in the case of each interpretation of suffering, there are people who like it and people who don't. And the very responses that some people find helpful may actually strike others as offensive.

Since different theodicies have different strengths, we may find ourselves drawing on a variety of resources in our efforts to develop a personal, practical response to suffering. And if we want to be helpful to others who suffer—and that may be the most important thing anyone can do—we need to remember that each perspective will appeal to some people and not to others. We may also find that a given theodicy can be helpful in meeting some forms of suffering,

---

[6]Viktor Frankl attributes this statement to Friedrich Nietzsche in *Man's Search for Meaning*, rev. ed. (New York: Washington Square, 1984), p. 97.

but much less helpful when it comes to others. And, while our discussion rests on the conviction that there are important connections between theory and practice, between theodicy and personal experience, it is important to remember that such connections are not airtight. A given theodicy may give expression or connect rather directly to certain responses to suffering, but this is hardly ever a *x* tidy, *if-then* logical connection. Only in rare instances do our sentiments and experiences perfectly reflect clear and distinct ideas. And while careful thinking can exert an influence on our perceptions and attitudes, seldom does it directly cause or produce them.

There is another reason for us to look at different theodicies. No single interpretation of suffering perfectly accounts for it. If, as we described it, a theodicy represents an attempt to map the experience of suffering, it is not surprising that each one leaves some of the territory uncharted. After all, no map perfectly represents the entire terrain it describes. No matter how much thought goes into our attempts to interpret the experience, a life-changing loss never makes perfect sense. There are always facets of the experience that defy comprehension.

For this reason, it would be more accurate for us to identify suffering as a mystery rather than a problem. As described by French philosopher Gabriel Marcel, a problem is an intellectual challenge that becomes more manageable, more comprehensible, the longer we think about it. In contrast, the more we contemplate a mystery, the more profound it becomes, the more it challenges our comprehension and resists a tidy explanation.[7] Clearly, the experience of suffering

---

[7]"A problem," to quote Gabriel Marcel, "is something which I meet, which I find complete before me, but which I can therefore lay siege to and reduce. But a mystery is something in which I myself am involved. . . . A genuine problem is subject to an appropriate technique by the exercise of which it is defined; whereas a mystery . . . transcends every conceivable technique." *The Mystery of Being*, vol. 1: *Reflection and Mystery*, trans. G. S. Fraser (Chicago: Henry Regnery, 1960), p. 260.

presents us with a mystery, not a problem. Even though interpretations of suffering are unavoidable, and the need for interpretation is urgent, we cannot expect a theodicy to meet all our practical needs nor to answer all our theoretical questions. As we examine different theodicies, it is therefore important for us to note the questions each one raises, in particular the questions that it leaves unanswered.

The Road Ahead

As we begin our journey, then, there are several things we need to keep in mind. First, suffering is universal. In one form or another, suffering is all around us, and sooner or later it reaches everyone. Second, the urge to make sense of suffering is universal too. We have an instinctive desire—a deep-seated need, in fact—to come to terms with our suffering, to come up with some way to explain or account for it, as people have been doing since the dawn of history. And third, no response to suffering is entirely adequate. No theory or explanation for suffering perfectly accounts for it, and no explanation is universally appealing. Every theodicy has its attractions and every theodicy raises questions. So we need to look at a variety of theodicies, and we need to look at all sides of each one— practical as well as theoretical, negative as well as positive.

In the following pages, we will survey seven different responses to suffering, noting both the personal appeal that each one exerts as well as the rationale that its supporters provide. We will also pay attention to the apparent limitations of each position, noting the questions it raises and seems to leave unanswered. While we will attempt to be fair in our descriptions, we will have to be content with a sketch of each position, rather than a fleshed-out portrait. Because we want to review a number of positions and bring them into conversation with each other, the scope of our inquiry is too broad to give any of them their due.

After all, we are dealing with issues that philosophers and theologians have been studying for centuries. Every position we will look at has been analyzed, criticized, indeed scrutinized, for years. Virtual mountains of books and articles have accumulated around each of them. Consequently, specialists who read the discussions in the following chapters, if any of them do, will no doubt find them relatively unsophisticated, especially if they have made our topic the object of their own extensive study. Nevertheless, there is still room for more accessible treatments of our topic. Everyone has a stake in the issues that suffering raises.

We sometimes say that war is too important to be left to the generals. In a somewhat similar way, theodicy is too important to be left to professionals. Because suffering comes to everyone sooner or later, we all face the challenge of trying to make sense of it. We can learn a great deal from philosophers and theologians who write about suffering, but we need not feel they are the only ones entitled to consider it. Because it seeks to join the practical with the theoretical, a discussion like ours can have great value.

The ultimate goal of our efforts is a personal one. In the final chapter we will assemble the insights gained along the way in the effort to construct a practical theodicy—a response to suffering that can stand up to thoughtful analysis and, more importantly, provide a source of strength in the midst of our own suffering. We hope to draw from our reflections some ideas that will help us, and help us help others when the unavoidable invades our lives and we face the question that never goes away.

2

GOD NEVER MAKES MISTAKES

Perfect Plan Theodicy

I SPOKE AT A CHURCH AN HOUR'S DRIVE from our home several years ago, and afterward my wife and I went to a friend's house for dinner. There was quite a group there and during the meal a lively discussion developed about the way God works in our lives. One young couple had returned from their honeymoon not long before, and the two were clearly enthralled with the joy of their new situation. "I am so happy now," the husband said. "I know for sure that God has been directing my life every single step of the way."

Then he told us some of the things he had been through. As a teenager, he got involved in drugs. To support his habit, he started dealing. That got him into trouble with the law. He went into recovery, though, cleaned up his life, got a job, met the girl of his dreams, and now he couldn't be happier. "Looking back on it all," he said, "I know that everything that happened to me is part of God's plan for my life." Another dinner guest suggested that a few of those things were not what God really intended, and that God blessed him in spite of them. But he was insistent. "No. God was leading me every step of the way. Everything I went through was just what God wanted.

He couldn't have brought me to where I am now by any other path."

The idea that there is purpose in everything that happens to us is a source of great strength to many people who suffer. They take comfort in the thought that everything that happens to them, in particular their sufferings and setbacks, are part of God's plan for their lives. In fact, some of the most ardent advocates of this view are people who have faced some tremendous losses.

In 1967, Joni Eareckson, an athletic teenager who had just graduated from high school, dived into the murky water of the Chesapeake Bay. She felt her head strike something hard, followed by a number of strange sensations. Her body sprawled out of control, she heard a loud electric buzzing and she floundered in the sand at the bottom of the bay. When someone finally pulled her to the surface, she gasped for air and realized to her horror that she couldn't move her arms and legs.

An ambulance rushed her to the hospital. After an emergency room visit, they moved her to the ICU and placed her motionless body on a Stryker frame so they could change her position every couple of hours. Within a few days she came to understand what had happened to her and what the future held. She had broken her neck between the fourth and fifth cervical vertebrae. She would be a quadriplegic for the rest of her life.

It has been decades since Joni's accident. Her story is known to millions of people. She's been interviewed on national television a number of times. She's learned how to draw with a pencil in her teeth and has become a successful artist. She eventually married Ken Tada, a high school political science teacher. She heads Joni and Friends, an organization devoted to helping people with physical challenges like her own. She has also written several dozen books—her autobiography sold over three million copies—and received numerous awards, including two honorary doctorates. In short, her life has been rich and full and a powerful influence for good.

The heart of Joni's story is her relationship with God. And the center of her relationship with God is a strong sense of divine sovereignty. She was nominally religious before the accident. But in the months that followed, under the influence of caring friends, she came to a much deeper experience. Over the years, Joni has faced her challenges with the powerful conviction that her life is the fulfillment of a plan that is perfect in all its details. "I began to see a mature purpose in all His dealings with me," she wrote in 1976.[1] She views her sufferings as opportunities to praise God, cultivate Christlike qualities of character, and bring comfort and encouragement to others. In her autobiography she emphatically asserts, "I wouldn't change my life for anything."[2]

This understanding of God's plan receives a fuller explanation in *When God Weeps,* a book Joni coauthored with Steven Estes. Quoting several Bible texts that say that "God does what he pleases" (cf. Dan 4:35; Ps 115:3), the authors conclude that when the Bible says that God permits or allows something, it does not mean that God stands back and lets things take their natural course. It actually refers to a specific divine intention. "When God allows something, he is acting deliberately—he is decreeing that event."[3] "Unless the Bible is wrong," they write, "*nothing* happens outside of God's decree. Nothing good, nothing bad, nothing pleasant, nothing tragic. . . . We may not fathom God's reasons . . . we may love him for it, we may hate him for it. But in simple language, God runs the world."[4]

---

[1] Joni Eareckson Tada, *Joni: An Unforgettable Story* (1976; repr., Grand Rapids: Zondervan, 2001), p. 173.
[2] Ibid., p. 188.
[3] Joni Eareckson Tada and Steven Estes, *When God Weeps: Why Our Sufferings Matter to the Almighty* (Grand Rapids: Zondervan, 1997), p. 82. Estes wrote the chapters in which the quoted statements appear.
[4] Ibid., p. 76.

"Do we find repulsive a God who gives the nod to our tragedies?" they ask. Emphatically, "No." The alternative is a God with one hand tied behind his back. If God "*didn't* deliberately permit the smallest details of your particular sorrows" and "screen our trials," then the world would be much worse than it is. "If God didn't control evil, the result would be evil uncontrollable." And if, instead of deliberately planning them, God merely reacts to sufferings after they occur or "patches things up," then our sufferings have no meaning and God is nothing more than "Satan's clean-up boy."[5] For those who take this position, then, God directs the course of human events in detail, and suffering plays an integral role in fulfilling God's purposes.

David and Janet Wilkins, a physician and his wife in Southern California, suffered a parent's worst nightmare when Swissair Flight 111 crashed into the Atlantic Ocean off the coast of Nova Scotia on September 2, 1998, killing all on board. One of the passengers was their son Monte, youngest of their four children, who was on his way to spend a year at a college in France. Since David Wilkins was a college classmate of mine, and since my daughter had flown to France just a few years earlier to study at the same school, this ca-tastrophe struck close to home.

Losing Monte was a watershed experience for the Wilkins family. That day sent them all on a challenging, painful and strangely re-warding journey. David Wilkins talks to groups fairly often and wrote a book describing the crash and its aftermath. After a lot of serious reflection, he eventually reached a position similar to the one described in *When God Weeps*. He came to the settled conviction that God is firmly in charge of everything that happens. In his words, "We serve a God who controls the world and all the coincidences."[6]

---

[5]Ibid., pp. 83-84.
[6]David Wilkins with Cecil Murphey, *United by Tragedy: A Father's Story* (Nampa, ID: Pacific Press, 2003), p. 137.

David's wife Janet was comfortable from the beginning accepting God's complete control of everything that comes to us and those we love. "She's absolutely sure that whatever touches our lives is His ultimate plan and would never exceed what we could bear."[7] But it was hard for Dave to accept this position himself. "I had to get past resenting God for allowing the situation to happen. I wanted to fight Him as I demanded answers. I wanted to believe that God was in control of my life and everything in the universe. If He was in control, how could this terrible ordeal have taken place? . . . It took a long time—maybe two years—before I finally was fully at peace with God being in charge of everything in this world."[8]

As David describes his journey, an important turning point in his thinking occurred when Cecil Murphey, his coauthor, asked him this question as they worked on the book. "Dave," he said, "just how sovereign is your God?" As Dave reflected on that question over time, he became convinced that he had underestimated God's sovereignty. A truly sovereign God, he came to believe, must exercise complete control over the world. And we can trust God's perfect plan, no matter how painful its details may be.

Something else that led David to this conclusion was his discovery that Monte's life had blessed others in ways he only came to know as time went by. During the year before he died, Monte had had a deeply religious experience. A number of young people told the Wilkinses about the powerful influence for good that Monte had been in their lives. Even people who learned about Monte only after he died were inspired by his story. As the evidence mounted, David realized that "Monte's life, although brief, had pleased God.

---

[7]Ibid., p. 118.
[8]Ibid., p. 90.

There had been no mistake."[9] Monte had fulfilled God's purpose for him. He didn't die one minute before he was meant to.

PERFECT PLAN THEODICY

The concept of a divine plan, universal in scope, perfect in every detail, brings great comfort to people. It gives them the strength to cope with enormous losses, physical and emotional, serenely confident in God's abiding love and tender care, certain that nothing happens outside God's will. The testimonies of people like Joni Eareckson Tada and David Wilkins are eloquent evidence of its power. We have to take seriously the views of those who speak from the depths of unimaginable pain and declare that God is good and that they have found in God an unfailing source of strength. There are several factors that make perfect plan theodicy appealing.

For one thing, it has impressive biblical support. There are numerous passages that portray God majestically directing the course of creaturely events. None is more impressive that the first chapter of the Bible. According to Genesis 1, God creates the world simply by speaking it into existence. The heavens, the earth and all that is in them have their origin in God's creative power. Numerous Psalms echo this theme, such as Psalm 104, which exclaims,

> O LORD, how manifold are your works!
> In wisdom you have made them all;
> the earth is full of your creatures. (Ps 104:24)

The theme continues in the prophets. Isaiah, for example, portrays God as presiding over all that happens in the world:

> It is he who sits above the circle of the earth,
> and its inhabitants are like grasshoppers;

---

[9]Ibid., p. 127.

who stretches out the heavens like a curtain,
and spreads them like a tent to live in;
who brings princes to naught,
and makes the rulers of the earth as nothing. (Is 40:22-23)

And God can bring about whatever God wants to happen.

I am God, and there is no other;
I am God, and there is no one like me,
declaring the end from the beginning
and from ancient times things not yet done,
saying, "My purpose shall stand,
and I will fulfill my intention," . . .
I have spoken, and I will bring it to pass;
I have planned, and I will do it. (Is 46:9-11)

There are also biblical passages that describe God's relation to the intimate details of our lives. The most famous verse in the Bible is probably Psalm 23:1: "The LORD is my shepherd, I shall not want." And it is just one of many statements offering assurance that God provides for God's people whatever their circumstances. The verse most frequently cited by those who believe that God's plan includes everything that happens to us is no doubt Romans 8:28: "All things work together for good for those who love God, who are called according to his purpose." Another is Jesus' assurance that not one sparrow "will fall to the ground apart from your Father" (Mt 10:29).

From this statement in Matthew and other passages, theologian Henri Blocher draws this conclusion: "Scripture never doubts God's command over every event, or that he determines everything that happens, in its entirety and in minutest detail: God is sovereign totally, radically, absolutely." The Bible, Blocher asserts, attributes to God "not only the course of nature and the overall march of history, but also the most personal events. . . . God's care extends even to the minutest occurrences."[10]

The idea also makes good sense. It follows logically from the conviction that God has infinite power and infinite wisdom. God can do anything God chooses, and God always chooses what's best. So whatever happens in this world is for the best. It happens because God wants it to.

The idea that God is in complete control, that everything that happens to us is part of God's perfect plan for our lives, also has significant personal appeal. It erases those nagging "what if?" questions. What if Joni had jumped into the water that day, instead of diving? What if Monte's original flight had been delayed and Flight 111 had taken off without him? How different so many lives would have been if just one small factor had changed. But with the perfect plan theodicy, there is no basis for second guessing and no reason for regret or self-reproach.

People appeal to the idea of a perfect plan not only to account for their own suffering. It is even more common for them to apply it to the suffering of others. Several years ago a seminary student stopped by my office with some questions about a book I had written on divine providence. After half an hour or so, he turned from theological issues to a pressing personal concern. "Let me tell you my most important reason for wanting to talk about this topic," he said. "Last year my wife and I were involved in a terrible traffic accident, and she died from her injuries. Afterward a number of people assured me that it must have been God's will for her life to end at that moment. After all, they said, a great many things had to happen precisely as they did, or the collision would not have

---

[10]Henri Blocher, *Evil and the Cross: An Analytical Look at the Problem of Pain*, trans. David G. Preston (Grand Rapids: Kregel, 1994), pp. 90-91.

occurred. 'It couldn't have been an accident,' people tell me. 'The odds are too great. There was a purpose behind it. It must have been part of God's definite plan for your lives."' My visitor didn't reveal his own interpretation of the loss, but he was clearly impressed with the explanation he had heard.

This "perfect plan theodicy," the idea that everything happens just the way God wants it to, appeals to our deep desire for order. It eliminates the yawning fear that life is capricious, that it's just a matter of chance whether terrible things happen—or don't happen—to us. And if chance is the ultimate explanation, then there is really no explanation. There is no rhyme or reason for anything. Indeed, to attribute our sufferings to blind chance, many believe, adds insult to injury. To bear them we need the assurance that they contribute to the meaning and purpose of our lives. And the concept that they are part of God's perfect plan for our lives provides this reassurance.

THE THEOLOGICAL BACKSTORY TO PERFECT PLAN THEODICY

Perfect plan theodicy goes hand in hand with the idea that the universe at every moment and in every detail is the precise expression of God's will. If God is God, the reasoning goes, divine sovereignty must be absolute. From every molecule to every galaxy, the entire scheme of things is exactly what God wants it to be.

Over the centuries people have taken various paths to this conclusion, but one of the most familiar is associated with the Protestant Reformation of the sixteenth century. The big issue behind this religious revolution in the Western church was the question of assurance. How can I know I'm saved? Martin Luther, the pivotal figure in the movement, entered a monastery as a young man, hoping to gain salvation, and faithfully submitted to the rigors of monastic life. But it brought no peace. As the years went by, he felt less and less hopeful that God would accept him.

When his superiors ordered him to teach, Luther began to study the Bible, and there he finally found the assurance he longed for. The key was Paul's message of righteousness by faith. When he realized that Paul's expression, "the righteousness of God," referred not to God's own righteousness but to the righteousness he gives to sinful human beings, Luther said the gates of paradise opened. He finally realized that we are saved, not by anything we do, not by any effort of our own, but entirely by the grace of God.

Because we are saved entirely by God's grace, Luther and the other great Reformers reasoned, human activity of any sort has nothing to contribute to the experience. Accordingly, even our response to God is not our own. Faith is not a decision we make for ourselves, it is something God decides for us.

In the best known section of his *Institutes of the Christian Religion*, John Calvin carries the irreversible priority of God's saving activity to its logical conclusion. He defines "predestination" as "the eternal decree of God, by which he determined with himself whatever he wished to happen with regard to every man. . . . Some are preordained to eternal life, others to eternal damnation . . . each has been created for one or other of these ends."[11]

We can be sure of our salvation, therefore, because God has decreed it, and nothing we do affects God's decision. A number of years ago two students at Princeton Theological Seminary described their gratitude for the doctrine this way. "Ironic as it sounds, accepting predestination into our lives was the most freeing thing that had ever happened to us spiritually. . . . We no longer had the burden of trying to be the Creator."[12]

---

[11]John Calvin, *Institutes of the Christian Religion* 3.21.5, Library of Christian Classics, vols. 20-21, ed. John T. MacNeill, trans. Ford Lewis Battles (Philadelphia: Westminster Press, 1960).

[12]Jennifer L. Bayne and Sarah E. Hinlicky, "Free to Be Creatures Again," *Christianity Today*, October 23, 2000, p. 44.

Not everyone who accepts the concept of predestination in the area of personal salvation applies it to everything else in the universe,[13] but many people do. Chapter three of the Westminster Confession of 1646 begins with these words, "God from all eternity did, by the most wise and holy counsel of his own will, freely and unchangeably ordain whatsoever comes to pass."

Perfect plan theodicy has a natural home in the overarching vision that God exercises absolute control over the world. Everything that happens, pleasant or painful, is exactly what God intends, and God never makes mistakes.

QUESTIONS ABOUT PERFECT PLAN THEODICY

As we shall see, every theodicy has its supporters and its detractors, and perfect plan theodicy is no exception. While some take great comfort in the thought that suffering fits nicely within God's perfect design, others find it difficult to accept, and some even find the idea abhorrent.

We might expect this theodicy to appeal to people whose losses have been minimal, or at least manageable, thinking perhaps that some forms of suffering might be easier to fit within the framework of divine purpose than others. As we have seen, however, it is also embraced by people whose losses are horrific. But in spite of its appeal to a wide range of sufferers, the idea that everything comes from God generates profound misgivings.

The most persistent challenge to perfect plan theodicy arises

---

[13]Calvinist theologians invoke a variety of distinctions regarding God's will, particularly to avoid implicating God in creaturely guilt. Thus Millard J. Erickson's "moderately Calvinistic model" distinguishes "God's general intention," or God's wish (i.e., "the values with which he is pleased"), from "God's specific intention in a given situation, what he decides shall actually occur." Thus "there are times . . . when God wills to permit, and thus to have occur, what he really does not wish. This is the case with sin." *Christian Theology* (Grand Rapids: Baker, 1983), 1:361.

from the fact that the world contains such massive amounts of suffering. It isn't hard for us to think of things that would lessen the world's pain—less disease, less hunger, less war, less crime and fewer natural disasters, for example—so one has to wonder why a God of infinite wisdom and love doesn't place more limits on the amount of evil that surrounds us. Couldn't a being who is infinite in wisdom and power achieve his or her purposes in less painful ways? Since its discovery in the early eighties, AIDS-related illnesses have claimed well over thirty million lives. And the twentieth century as a whole, for example, is sometimes referred to as "the century of death," because it saw human beings kill one another at an incomprehensible rate. The estimates run as high as 120 million. The Holocaust, in particular, is a source of persistent perplexity. And for some, it transposes the problem of suffering into an entirely novel key. What sort of divine plan could possibly involve the systematic extermination of six million people? How could anyone view such cruelty as part of something good?

The same question applies to certain forms of suffering on an individual scale. Several years ago, a young woman I had known since her childhood was raped and murdered just as she was finishing her education and starting her career. I have never heard her parents describe her death as part of God's plan for her. It is hard to imagine them doing so. The death of every young person is tragic, but some are particularly wrenching. It is difficult to fit deliberate, fatal violence into a perfect master plan.

As we noted in chapter one, each thoughtful response to suffering exhibits an enduring personal attraction. There are people who find it genuinely helpful in facing the losses life brings to them. At the same time, there is no unencumbered theodicy. Alongside each of them we find persistent questions, nagging doubts. For some people, the attraction of a particular theodicy is so strong that they can live with the questions. For others, the doubts are too much. They look for other ways of conceiving God's relation to a suffering world.

If theodicy were a mere intellectual exercise, we could react as we do with many unresolved issues. We could leave the problem to the experts, let them look for solutions and wait to hear from them when they find one. When it comes to suffering, however, as we observed in chapter one, the exigencies of life do not allow us that luxury. The quest for a theodicy is not an academic diversion; it is driven by an urgent personal need. Because suffering is unavoidable, theodicy is inescapable. Because we cannot live without a sense that our lives make sense, and suffering threatens that confidence, we must find a way to recover, rescue or rehabilitate it. And while no theodicy perfectly answers all the questions that suffering brings, looking at the options may help us find a way to respond to suffering resourcefully when we most need it.

None of the responses to suffering we will look at attracts more ardent support or more robust criticism than perfect plan theodicy. Its enduring appeal is the assurance it provides that nothing that ever happens can thwart God's will for us, because everything that happens is somehow part of God's will. We can rest secure in the thought that whatever life brings to us, it is essential to God's purposes for us. Because the very concept that some find so attractive raises serious doubts in others, we need to look at other ways of responding to suffering as well.

3

LET FREEDOM RING

The Free Will Defense

A FORMER COLLEAGUE OF MINE in her mid-thirties discovered she had ovarian cancer the day her second child was born. Sharon Harris began treatment immediately, and several weeks later I got a letter that she and her husband Jim sent to their friends and relatives to tell them how things were going. The letter reported on the progress of her illness and the medical care she was receiving. It described the ways their lives had changed. It told how the two of them, their children and their parents were coping with all the challenges they faced. The letter also mentioned some of the things people had said to them when they heard about Sharon's illness—things like, "Everything happens for a purpose," "God is testing your faith," "God never sends us more than we can bear"—all statements reflecting the conviction that their situation was something that fit nicely within God's plan. However well-meaning their speakers were, Jim and Sharon did not find these sentiments at all helpful. In fact, they found them deeply troubling. The letter closed with this paragraph:

We also feel we must say without reservation that we believe this experience is *not* God's will. We understand that we live in a world full of evil and we accept that. However, to suggest that God is somehow responsible or involved in this implies a God that is harsher than any of you. The Scriptures suggest that Jesus could not pass by any suffering without stopping to alleviate that pain. Since God is even more loving than us (we would not wish this experience even on our worst enemy), we understand God to be working in the healing process, certainly not in the process that resulted in cancer.

Jim and Sharon's letter raises one of the most important questions people can ask about our topic. Does suffering take place "inside" or "outside" God's will? Is suffering something God wants for us, or is it opposed to God's purposes? For those who embrace perfect plan theodicy, as we saw in chapter two, God's will encompasses everything that happens, including life's most painful experiences. Others, in contrast, are compelled to place suffering outside God's will. Sharon and Jim found no comfort in the idea that her cancer was something God wanted for them. And the suggestion that God was somehow behind their ordeal only made things worse. What strengthened them was the thought that the illness threatening her life was not at all what God wanted, indeed, that it was emphatically opposed to God's will.

The fact that people respond to suffering in such different ways, and that no single theodicy is universally appealing, shows how important it is to consider a range of interpretations. The basic idea that God is not responsible for the world's suffering, that it lies outside God's will for the creatures, appears in a number of different theodicies. One of the most influential among them is generally known as "the free will defense."

FREEDOM AND DIVINE RESPONSIBILITY

When we ask if suffering lies inside or outside God's will, indeed if anything that happens could ever go against God's will, our attention immediately goes to the one divine attribute that everybody thinks about when they suffer, namely, God's power. "If God is so powerful," sufferers are bound to wonder, "why is this happening to me? If God has the power to end my suffering, why doesn't God use it?" What philosophers typically call "the problem of evil" frames the issue this way: A God who is perfect in goodness would want to eliminate evil, and a God who is perfect in power would be able to eliminate it. Yet evil exists. So it must be the case that God is either less than perfect in goodness, or less than perfect in power, or perhaps less than perfect in both. Once in a while, people call the goodness of God into question[1]—on some interpretations, the biblical figure of Job does this[2]—but that's a rare exception. In one way or another, most theodicies, including the ones we will examine in this and most of the following chapters, focus on the question of divine power. Just what does perfect power involve? How much of what goes on in the world is God responsible for?

As most philosophers describe it, "omnipotence," or infinite power, is one of God's distinctive qualities. Indeed, the attribute of supreme power seems essential to the very meaning of the word *God*. It refers to God's ability to do anything, to bring about any state of affairs God wants to.[3] And this raises an obvious question

---

[1]See, for example, John K. Roth, "A Theodicy of Protest," in *Encountering Evil: Live Options in Theodicy*, ed. Stephen T. Davis (Atlanta: John Knox, 1981), pp. 7-22, 30-37.

[2]According to Harold Kushner, for example, it is Job's position that God is not supremely good. God refuses to be held accountable to human standards. "God is so powerful that He is not limited by considerations of fairness and justice." *When Bad Things Happen to Good People* (New York: Schocken Books, 1981), p. 40.

[3]In the words of philosopher Richard Swinburne, "God is omnipotent in that whatever he chooses to do, he succeeds in doing." *The Christian God* (New York: Oxford University Press, 1994), p. 129. "What the theist claims about God is that he [has] power to create,

for those who place suffering outside God's will. Why, if God is supremely powerful, does God allow suffering in the world God made? If God can do anything God chooses, and if suffering is opposed to God's will, why doesn't God get rid of it? Even better, why didn't God prevent it in the first place?

Over the years, many Christian thinkers have responded to this question with one simple answer: *free will.* There is suffering in the world, they say, because some of God's creatures misused their freedom. God gave certain creatures the capacity to make important choices, in particular the choice to give or withhold their loyalty to God, to obey or disobey God's commands. Sadly, they disregarded God's directives, and the world's ills are ultimately the result of their rebellion. Suffering, then, is a consequence of sin, and sin is a misuse of freedom.[4]

There are numerous biblical passages that underscore the importance of freedom, and a number of them connect suffering to the willful decision to disobey God.[5] It occupies a prominent place in the biblical accounts of creation. According to Genesis 2, God

---

conserve, or annihilate anything, big or small. . . . God is not limited by the laws of nature; he makes them and he can change or suspend them—if he chooses. To use the technical term, God is omnipotent: he can do anything." *Is There a God?* (New York: Oxford University Press, 1996), pp. 5-6.

[4]The sort of freedom envisioned here is sometimes identified as "libertarian freedom"— freedom, that is, to do otherwise. Richard Swinburne describes it this way: "I understand by a being's having free will that he acts intentionally and that how he acts is not fully determined by prior states of the world; his choices are to some extent up to him." *The Existence of God* (Oxford: Clarendon, 1979), p. 153. There are other conceptions of freedom, of course, including what is sometimes called "compatibilist freedom," according to which a person may be free even though his/her future actions are certain. See Antony Flew, "Compatibilism, Free Will and God," *Philosophy* 48 (1973): 231-32; cited in Millard J. Erickson, *Christian Theology* (Grand Rapids: Baker, 1985), 1:357.

[5]For example, Joshua made this stirring appeal to the ancient Israelites after they had entered the Promised Land: "Choose this day whom you will serve . . . but as for me and my household, we will serve the LORD" (Josh 24:15). Centuries later, the prophet Ezekiel bore this message to God's people, "Say to them, As I live, says the LORD GOD, I have no pleasure in the death of the wicked, but that the wicked turn from their ways and live; turn back, turn back from your evil ways; for why will you die, O house of Israel?" (Ezek 33:11).

created Adam and put him in the Garden of Eden. Then God said, "You may freely eat of every tree of the garden; but of the tree of the knowledge of good and evil you shall not eat, for in the day that you eat of it you shall die" (Gen 2:16-17). As generally interpreted, this command implies that Adam and Eve were free to obey or disobey God's command. In other words, it was up to them to determine whether or not they would remain loyal to God.

The next chapters of Genesis record their act of disobedience and its consequences. They ate the forbidden fruit, they lost their Eden home, and the trials that we are all too familiar with ensued— physical challenges (pain and toil), emotional turmoil (one of their sons killed the other) and ultimately death. For many people, this narrative sounds a note that reverberates throughout the Bible: the origin of suffering lies in human misdeeds—the misuse of our God-given freedom—rather than a divine design. It is our willful violation of what we're meant to do and be that ultimately accounts for the ills that afflict us.

From this perspective, God is not responsible for the mistakes humans make, nor for the sufferings that these mistakes lead to, because God is not the only one who contributes to the course of events. This is how Old Testament scholar Terence Fretheim describes this relationship: "God lets the creation be what it was created to be, without micromanagement, tight control, or interference every time something goes wrong. . . . God's creation does not preclude creaturely possibilities that are negative, even anticreational."[6]

The "free will defense," as it is generally called, relieves God of responsibility for suffering by placing it squarely on the creatures. Once God created beings who were endowed with freedom, the

---

[6]Terence E. Fretheim, *God and World in the Old Testament: A Relational Theology of Creation* (Nashville: Abingdon, 2005), p. 7.

argument goes, God was no longer responsible for everything that happens in the world. From that point on, the decisions of the creatures were genuinely *their* decisions, not God's, and they could do what they chose with the freedom they were given, whether it pleased God or not. So, when creaturely freedom enters the picture, the course of events is not the sole result of God's will. It is determined by God *and* the creatures, not by God alone.

Philosopher Alvin Plantinga applies this notion of shared responsibility to the question of evil in this oft-cited summary of the free will defense:

> A world containing creatures who are significantly free (and freely perform more good than evil actions) is more valuable, all else being equal, than a world containing no free creatures at all. Now God can create free creatures, but He can't *cause* or *determine* them to do only what is right. For if He does so, then they aren't significantly free after all; they do not do what is right *freely*. To create creatures capable of *moral good,* therefore, He must create creatures capable of moral evil; and He can't give these creatures the freedom to perform evil and at the same time prevent them from doing so.... The fact that free creatures sometimes go wrong, however, counts neither against God's omnipotence nor against His goodness; for He could have forestalled the occurrence of moral evil only by removing the possibility of moral good.[7]

This explanation emphasizes both the nature and importance of freedom. As Plantinga describes it, moral freedom is the capacity to make an uncoerced choice between significant alternatives. In other words, it is a genuinely personal act—an act for which a

---

[7]Alvin C. Plantinga, *God, Freedom, and Evil* (Grand Rapids: Eerdmans, 1974), p. 30, italics original.

person himself or herself is responsible. Consequently, a free act cannot be brought about or caused by anyone or anything else, for in that case it would not be the actor's own choice.

The effect of the free will defense, then, is to stop responsibility for suffering one step short of God. Evil originated with the creatures, not with the Creator. True, God created beings and endowed them with personal freedom, but God is not responsible for what they did with their freedom. To put it another way, God is responsible for the *possibility* of evil, but not for the *actuality* of evil. The creatures who misused their freedom are entirely to blame for that.

But why would God create beings with the ability to do things God really didn't want them to do? Why would God give anyone that kind of power? The answer to this question lies in the nature of divine love. According to a number of important biblical statements, love is the most fundamental, indeed, the defining attribute of God. The most famous verse in the New Testament begins with the affirmation, "God so loved the world" (Jn 3:16). And another verse, which comes as close as any statement in the Bible to a definition of God, declares, "God is love" (1 Jn 4:8).

Because God creates out of love, and because God desires a relationship with the creatures that is characterized by love, God is not satisfied with mere obedience. God wants the creatures to be loyal to God because they choose to be. Because God's very nature is to love, God seeks to be loved, so God created beings who could return God's love for them. Love, however, requires freedom. God's creatures would not be free to say yes to God unless they were free to say no. Sadly, this is just what some of them did.

For perfect plan theodicy, God's infinite power guarantees that everything fulfills God's purposes. God can achieve God's purposes unilaterally, so to speak. Nothing interferes with the fulfillment of God's plans. For the free will defense, God's purposes require the cooperation of the creatures. And because the creatures are free, they may or may not decide to cooperate. From the perfect plan perspective, the world we live in is the way God wants it to be—not the way it will ultimately be, perhaps, but the way God wants it to be now. From the free will perspective, in contrast, the world we live in now is not the world God wants. It's a "fallen world." It is a drastic departure from God's ideal.

The difference in these views of creation leads to a striking difference in their views of suffering. From the perfect plan perspective, suffering is part of God's overall design. For the free will defense, suffering conflicts with God's objectives. There is a drastic difference between what God wanted for the creatures and what they chose for themselves. Instead of freely returning God's love, they freely rejected it, and suffering is the consequence of this terrible mistake.

THE ATTRACTIONS OF THE FREE WILL DEFENSE

Many people find the free will defense attractive because it seems to fit our intuitive reaction to suffering so well. When something terrible occurs, our feelings tell us that it should never have happened. It is simply wrong. My niece died unexpectedly when she was only nineteen. My sister and her husband received stacks of sympathy cards. But one she particularly remembers came from one of her daughter's friends. The sender had simply written, "Oh no," and signed her name. *Oh no!* It's the shortest, most poignant response to a great loss. The free will defense assures us that we are entitled to those feelings. God never meant for us to suffer. It was not something God intended for us. Consequently, we have every right to resent it, resist it, relieve it and try to eliminate it.

It is helpful to remember other facets of freedom in this connection too. For one, freedom is more than just the capacity to select from various options. In other words, it involves more than the mere act of choosing. It also involves having the results of our choices play out, so to speak. Significant choices have significant consequences. And we find our lives embedded in an intricate network of cause and effect whose elements cannot be attributed directly to God. To be sure, God may be active in the world, intimately aware of and intensely concerned about everything that happens to us, but God is not by any means the only factor that determines the course of history or shapes the pattern of our lives.

Along with the capacity to make significant choices, in particular to choose whether or not to accept God's love, God also granted the creatures the capacity to love one another, to interact with and influence each other in profoundly significant ways. It is one of life's great privileges to contribute to the lives of other people and to receive their contributions to ours. Indeed, there are values that we can realize only in cooperation with other persons. As Richard Swinburne observes, "Our world is clearly arranged so that men working together can bring about goals which working separately they cannot."[8] But this arrangement comes with a price. A world where people are genuinely affected by what others decide and do is also a world where people can do each other harm. And the greater the good they can achieve, the more damaging the harm they can do. Here again, people can exercise freedom to do radically different things.

Recognizing that we are genuinely affected, for good and for ill, by the decisions and actions of other people, and that these were genuinely their own choices, not necessarily something God intended, prevents us from blaming God for difficulties that others may create for us.

---

[8]Swinburne, *Existence of God,* p. 187.

Not long ago, I listened as two people I know, a sister and brother, shared some reflections on their childhood. They had a difficult home situation during their early years. Their father struggled with drug and alcohol addiction, and this naturally affected their mother's health. The two were convinced that their parents loved them—they never felt neglected or abandoned. And their parents worked to provide the semblance of a stable home as long as they could until they eventually divorced. But the stress these two endured during their childhood had lasting effects. At the same time, the passage of time has enlarged their perspective on their parents' lives as well. Looking back, they realize that both their parents came from less than ideal homes themselves, and that may well have contributed to the problems they encountered later on. The important decisions people make have important consequences, and sometimes these carry over generations.[9] The reality of personal freedom means that our lives will inevitably be affected, for good or ill, by the actions and decisions of other people, particularly those closest to us.

One of God's greatest gifts to human beings, the capacity to choose our destiny and to influence the lives of others, is therefore one of the most complicating factors in human life. It obliges us to recognize that God's will is not the only factor that accounts for what happens.

Questions About the Free Will Defense

Any time people talk about freedom, a lot of questions come up. So it is not surprising that this perspective on suffering has generated a great deal of discussion. The free will defense seeks to shift responsibility for suffering from God to the creatures, but some people insist that God is still responsible for suffering, even if the creatures

---

[9]Perhaps this is one way to construe biblical passages that speak of God keeping steadfast love for thousands of generations and "visiting the iniquity of the parents upon the children and the children's children, to the third and the fourth generation" (Ex 34:7).

are free. This is the argument one philosopher, J. L. Mackie, gives:

> If God has made men such that in their free choices they some-times prefer what is good and sometimes what is evil, why could he not have made men such that they always freely choose the good? If there is no logical impossibility in a man's freely choosing the good on one, or on several, occasions, there cannot be a logical impossibility in this freely choosing the good on every occasion. . . . There was open to [God] the . . . possibility of making beings who would act freely but always go right. Clearly, his failure to avail himself of this possibility is inconsistent with his being both omnipotent and wholly good.[10]

For Mackie, then, an all-powerful God could have created morally free beings who always choose to do good. But God didn't, and the failure to do so makes God responsible for evil and suffering. Supporters of the free will defense reply that Mackie's reasoning rests on an important oversight. It is logically possible for moral agents to choose the good in every situation, they admit. But it doesn't follow that God acting alone could make this happen—which is what Mackie assumes. A world where freedom exists and evil doesn't is not a possibility that God can bring about unilaterally. Only God *and* the creatures could achieve that.

Mackie's challenge underscores the fact that "omnipotence," or perfect power, needs to be defined with great care.[11] Perfect power

---

[10]J. L. Mackie, "Evil and Omnipotence," in *God and the Problem of Evil*, ed. William L. Rowe (Malden, MA: Blackwell, 2001), p. 86. Mackie's essay originally appeared in *Mind* 64, no. 254 (1955): 200-212, and has been anthologized numerous times.

[11]The books, chapters and articles devoted to the topic of omnipotence would fill a library, probably several libraries. Any discussion of the idea of God will take up the issues it raises. See, for example, Thomas V. Morris, *Our Idea of God: An Introduction to Philosophical Theology* (Downers Grove, IL: InterVarsity Press, 1991), which moves through successive qualifications from "God can do everything" to "Anything that it is logically possible for a perfect being to do, God can do," as an appropriate way to express divine omnipotence (pp. 66-68).

cannot mean simply, "God can do ____" (and then we just fill in the blank). Instead, most philosophers agree, it can only mean "power to do what is logically possible."[12] But this too needs further refinement. Omnipotence is not simply "the power to bring about any logical possibility." If God has endowed the creatures with the power of decision and self-determination, we need to revise the definition to read, "power to do anything logically possible *that does not require creaturely cooperation*." If there are logical possibilities that require creaturely cooperation, then God cannot realize them by acting alone.

According to another objection to the free will defense, freedom inevitably leads to suffering. If the world is populated with creatures who are free, someone sooner or later is bound to sin. It is statistically inevitable. Again, defenders of the free will defense find a flaw in this reasoning. Just because rebellion is possible, they reply, does not mean that it was inevitable, or even likely, to occur. Improbable things sometimes happen, and perhaps this was one of them. To be sure, suffering is so much a part of things now that we can't imagine the world without it. But conceivably there may have been a time when the possibility of suffering was remote. Yes, God made beings who were capable of turning away from God. But suppose God created them with a natural inclination to return God's love and then did everything possible to ensure that they would remain loyal, while still respecting their freedom.

There are also people who react to the free will defense by maintaining that good and evil necessarily go together. We wouldn't know what moral goodness is, they argue, unless evil existed alongside it. An early Christian writer explained it this way: The

---

[12]For Richard Swinburne, the claim that "God is omnipotent, that is, literally can do anything," needs the "obvious qualification that to be omnipotent a person need not be able to do the logically impossible." *The Coherence of Theism* (Oxford: Clarendon, 1977), p. 149.

tongue receives experience of sweet and bitter by means of tasting. The eye discriminates between black and white by means of vision. And the ear recognizes the distinctions of sounds by hearing. In a similar way, goes the argument, the mind comes to know good because it knows "the contrary." So without a knowledge of evil, there could be no knowledge of good.[13] If creatures are morally free, they must be able to choose between good and evil. And if evil is a genuine option, it must stand side by side with the good. The existence of evil is therefore essential to moral freedom. Without it, we would not be able to choose the good or even recognize the good.

The idea that moral goodness would be impossible unless evil goes with it has numerous supporters. But again, there are those who find fault with the idea. From their perspective, good and evil are not counterparts at all. Their status is vastly different. Goodness is essential to the nature of things, but evil isn't. In fact, strictly speaking, evil does not really "exist."

To follow their reasoning, think of some of the apple varieties you know. Your list would probably include names such as Golden Delicious, Fuji, Gala, Pink Lady and so on. Would you put "bad apple" on the list? Of course not. But why? We all know what bad apples are. We have all seen bad apples. But a bad apple is not another variety of apple, alongside Braeburn, Jonagold and the rest. Why not? Because a bad apple is not a different kind of apple. In fact, it is not a kind of apple at all. A bad apple is a good apple that has lost some of its goodness.

We find something like this in the writings of St. Augustine, the great church father. As he describes it, evil is not a thing or an entity that stands alongside other things in the world. To quote Edward Conlon, "St. Augustine said that evil was not a phenomenon in and

[13]Irenaeus, *Against Heresies*, 4.39.1. Quoted in John Hick, *Evil and the God of Love* (New York: Harper & Row, 1966), p. 214.

of itself, but an absence of good, much like cold and dark have no physical reality beyond the absence of light and heat."[14] Rightly understood, then, evil has no existence of its own. Nothing is evil, pure and simple. To call something "evil" is to say that some of its essential goodness has been taken away or corrupted. Evil, therefore, is nothing more than a corruption or "privation"—Augustine's word—of something that is originally good.

Those who adopt this view of evil also revise their concept of moral choice. People typically speak of moral freedom as the ability to choose between good and evil, but to those for whom evil as such does not, strictly speaking, exist, such language is misleading. If good and evil do not represent opposing entities, the real options facing God's creatures are not to turn toward good or turn toward evil. Instead, the options are to turn *toward* the good or *away* from the good. When it comes to evil, there is nothing, literally no thing, there to turn to.

While careful analysis reveals that evil has no reality of its own—or no positive ontological status, to use philosophical language—this does not mean that evil is merely imaginary. Far from it. We experience evil as a vivid, palpable presence in the world. The effects of sin, of turning away from God, are all too real, and sooner or later they reach us all. Moreover, the view that evil is a corruption of the good also reminds us that the greater someone's capacity for good is, the greater the evil of which he or she is capable. According to Christian tradition, to cite the most glaring example, the devil himself, the epitome of evil, is nothing less than a fallen angel, a creature who devotes his immense abilities to horrifying ends.

---

[14]Edward Conlon, *Blue Blood* (New York: Riverhead Books, 2004), p. 121. This succinct phrasing of Augustine appears in Conlon's widely read account of life as an officer in the New York City Police Department. You never know where you'll run into philosophical reflections!

Along with perfect plan theodicy, the free will defense is one of the most popular responses to suffering. The two also have a good deal in common. Both affirm that God is perfect in power and goodness. They agree that God created the world, that God cares for the world, that God has important plans for the world and that suffering is something God works to overcome. But they disagree as to the nature of God's relation to the world. They differ as to whether suffering is part of God's overall plan or something that is inherently opposed to it.

As our first two theodicies indicate, suffering generates a variety of responses and each response raises further questions. Philosophers and theologians have devoted vast amounts of time to reflecting on them, and their discussions can quickly become quite technical. But even if their language seems removed from ordinary life, the underlying issues never are. When it comes to suffering, the questions that occupy philosophers are questions that concern all of us. Suffering is something everyone faces, and it is something we all want answers to. In the chapters to come we will look at some of the other responses to this ever-present challenge.

4

NO PAIN, NO GAIN

Soul Making Theodicy

HAVE YOU EVER HAD A PAINFUL EXPERIENCE that turned out to be exactly what you needed?

Years ago the president of a company I was under contract to work for came to the school I was attending to discuss my future. He told me about the position he had decided to give me when I graduated a few months later. His announcement blew me away. The job was not only better than anything I had hoped for, it was better than anything I could have imagined. In fact, until he described it, I didn't even know such a position existed. Naturally, I could hardly wait to let everyone know about my good fortune. He said things weren't quite finalized, however, so I shouldn't tell anyone about it until the official letter came from his office.

It's hard to keep news like this to yourself, but I managed to do it. Partly, I suppose, because I knew how excited my family and how envious my friends would be. As the weeks went by, the suspense became almost unbearable. Each day I went to the mailbox with my heart pounding. Would the letter be there? No. Disappointment and then another twenty-four hours of mounting anticipation.

Finally, it arrived—the letter that would change my life. I held the magic envelope in my hands and read the address several times. There was only one problem. My wife wasn't at home to share the moment. After waiting all this time, I decided, I could wait a few more hours until she finished her shift at the hospital. When she finally arrived, we sat down in our little apartment. I ceremoniously opened the envelope and started to read. But my voice quickly trailed off. The job it told me I was going to get wasn't even close to the job I had been promised. After careful thought, the president wrote, the committee had decided that, relatively inexperienced as I was, I didn't have the qualifications necessary for the position. They had found someone better suited, and they were therefore giving me another assignment.

Was I disappointed? Much worse than that, I felt betrayed. Why had they treated me this way? Why had they even mentioned the dream job if there was any chance they wouldn't give it to me? And above all, I wondered, where was God in all of this? Why did God let someone play games with my life? I turned to my new responsibilities with a heavy heart.

It didn't take long for my perspective to change completely. Within a few weeks I realized that my "replacement" was far better suited for the job I was originally promised than I was. He had talents that I didn't. And the challenges he had to face were far more complicated and demanding than I could have known ahead of time. Had I gotten the position I was dreaming of, I soon realized, I would have been miserable. Furthermore, the assignment I did receive was not only more suited to my abilities, it made it possible for me to go on to things that were more rewarding in the long run. Where was God in the disappointment I had experienced? It was obvious. God was helping me learn and grow from the frustrations and setbacks that came my way.

While my temporary disappointment hardly qualifies as an example of suffering—it pales in comparison to the heart-rending tragedies that news reports bring us every day—the trajectory of my experience follows that of another influential response to life's losses. Many people have discovered that suffering has a great deal to teach us. Even our most painful experiences can be occasions for growth and development.

There are many biblical references to the suffering of the righteous, and different passages look at suffering from differing perspectives. A number of them acknowledge that suffering is pervasive among God's people, if not inevitable. Paul's letters contain vivid accounts of his own tribulations. An abbreviated list includes "afflictions, hardships, calamities, beatings, imprisonments, riots, labors, sleepless nights, hunger" (2 Cor 6:4-5). A longer account describes "countless floggings," several shipwrecks, danger from all sorts of people (bandits, his own people, Gentiles, false brothers and sisters) and in all sorts of places (in the city, in the wilderness, at sea), as well as being "often without food, cold and naked," and feeling anxiety and constant pressure (2 Cor 11:23-28). And according to a climactic passage in Paul's longest letter, suffering is not just something courageous apostles have to face, it is a challenge that confronts all who are children of God, "heirs of God and joint heirs with Christ": "we suffer with him so that we may also be glorified with him" (Rom 8:17).

Pervasive though it may be, suffering is also a source of great perplexity. If we live in a morally-ordered world, logic seems to require, good people should never have to suffer. Indeed, a repeated theme in the Bible's wisdom literature is that God's way is the best way, the sure path to a good life. The righteous will enjoy prosperity and longevity, while the wicked, those who ignore God's instruction, will be "like chaff that the wind drives away" (Ps 1:4). Sounds straightforward and encouraging, but life is much

more complicated, as other writings in the wisdom tradition acknowledge. According to the author of Ecclesiastes, there is no
ultimate difference between the two groups—"the same fate comes
to all, to the righteous and the wicked, to the good and the evil"
(Eccles 9:2). And in Job, the oldest book in the Bible, a conspicu-
ously righteous person suffers more intensely than anyone around
him, to his great consternation.

Why is there suffering in God's world, why does suffering come
to some people and not, apparently, to others, and why, most poignantly, does God allow *me* to suffer? We find all these questions in
the Bible: the cry of anguish in Psalm 22, "My God, my God, why
have you forsaken me? Why are you so far from helping me, from
the words of my groaning?"; the bewilderment expressed in Psalm
73 asking why the wicked prosper while the righteous suffer; the
question the curious disciples asked Jesus, just why was a certain
man born blind (Jn 9:2)?

Then there are statements in the Bible that put suffering in a positive light. Suffering should not be a source of perplexity, but a cause
for rejoicing. In 1 Peter, the apostle tells his readers, "Do not be
surprised at the fiery ordeal that is taking place among you to test
you, as though something strange were happening to you. But rejoice insofar as you are sharing Christ's sufferings, so that you may
also be glad and shout for joy when his glory is revealed. If you are
reviled for the name of Christ, you are blessed, because the spirit of
glory, which is the Spirit of God, is resting on you" (1 Pet 4:12-14).

Instead of diminishing us, suffering helps us grow. After all, even
Jesus learned "through what he suffered" (Heb 5:8). And the benefits
of suffering are significant. As Paul describes it, "suffering produces
endurance, and endurance produces character, and character produces hope" (Rom 5:3-4). And according to the book of Hebrews,
suffering is nothing less than a manifestation of divine care for us.

Endure trials for the sake of discipline. God is treating you as children; for what child is there whom a parent does not discipline? If you do not have that discipline in which all children share, then you are illegitimate and not his children. Moreover, we had human parents to discipline us, and we respected them. Should we not be even more willing to be subject to the Father of spirits and live? For they disciplined us for a short time as seemed best to them, but he disciplines us for our good, in order that we may share his holiness. Now, discipline always seems painful rather than pleasant at the time, but later it yields the peaceful fruit of righteousness to those who have been trained by it. (Heb 12:7-11)

In one of his letters, the apostle Paul recounts what he learned from an affliction he suffered, from something he calls "a thorn in the flesh."[1] "Three times," he states, "I appealed to the Lord about this, that it would leave me, but he said to me, 'My grace is sufficient for you, for power is made perfect in weakness.' So, I will boast all the more gladly of my weaknesses, so that the power of Christ may dwell in me. Therefore I am content with weaknesses, insults, hardships, persecutions, and calamities for the sake of Christ; for whenever I am weak, then I am strong" (2 Cor 12:8-10).

It doesn't take a distinctly religious perspective to see that suffering can be beneficial. It is a widespread conviction. In fact, some people believe that we can learn more from the difficulties and setbacks that come to us than from any other experience. In *My Losing Season*, Pat Conroy describes his disappointing final year on the varsity basketball team at the Citadel, the famous military academy in Charleston, South Carolina. The prologue concludes with these words:

---

[1]Scholars have never determined just what this "thorn" actually was.

Sports books are always about winning because winning is far more pleasurable and exhilarating to read about than losing. . . . Loss is a fiercer, more uncompromising teacher, coldhearted but clear-eyed in its understanding that life is more dilemma than game, and more trial than free pass. My acquaintance with loss has sustained me during the stormy passages of my life. . . . Though I learned some things from the games we won that year, I learned much, much more from loss.[2]

Even some of life's worst experiences can lead to positive results. In the acknowledgments he includes in his acclaimed biography of Francisco Goya, the great Spanish painter, Robert Hughes thanks a long list of people who helped him after a near-fatal accident in Western Australia. He underwent a dozen operations and spent six months in various hospitals, from Perth, Australia, to New York City. "Without all of these people . . . who looked after me," he concludes, "this book could never possibly have been written." Then he adds this reflection: "Perhaps, if life is fully experienced, there is no waste. It was through the accident that I came to know extreme pain, fear, and despair; and it may be that the writer who does not know fear, despair and pain cannot fully know Goya."[3] The depths of Hughes's own experience gave him insights into the work of the artist he would not otherwise have had.

Through enormous tragedies—excruciating pain, irreversible losses and near-fatal injuries—people evidently learn things about life, others and themselves they could learn in no other way. The discovery that the worst experiences can ultimately enhance our lives often comes as a surprise. As Darren Wilkins remarked to his

2Pat Conroy, *My Losing Season: A Memoir* (New York: Doubleday, 2002), p. 14.
3Robert Hughes, *Goya* (New York: Knopf, 2003), p. x.

father, David, in the aftermath of his brother's death, "Dad, this is the hardest thing I've ever been through. But it's also the richest."

According to "soul making theodicy," as it is often called, the value of moral growth or character development provides us with the best explanation for the presence of suffering in the world. From this perspective, it is not only possible for us to grow through suffering, suffering is absolutely essential to our growth. Without it we could never become everything we are meant to be. The lessons we most need to learn, the qualities of character we most need to acquire, are possible only if we undergo hardship and difficulty. To fulfill our potential, we therefore need the sort of environment that contains obstacles and challenges. And for this reason, the world as it presently exists, dangerous and threatening though it is, represents an ideal place for personal growth. It is the perfect setting for character development.

The Attraction of Soul Making Theodicy

This approach to suffering connects with a desire that lies deep within us to build a framework of meaning around our painful experiences. The sufferings we are concerned with in this book, "tsunamis of the soul," involve serious, life-changing loss—loss of such magnitude that there is no way to ignore, negate or reverse it. Loss that prevents any return to the world we lived in before. Loss so profound that it becomes part of our very identity. When people experience a loss of such magnitude, the question inevitably arises, does it negate the meaning of our lives? Does it empty them of all significance?

In spite of its undeniable and devastating power, there is something within people that refuses to succumb to suffering. We will not let it reduce us to helpless victims. Suffering may change us, we seem to say, but it need not destroy us. We need not bow to its tyranny or let it deprive our lives of significance. We have an instinctive desire to "rise above" our sufferings, to deny suffering the last word. Soul making theodicy supports this response. Far from destroying the meaning of life, this theodicy assures us, suffering can actually help us to find it.

Soon after the bombings that marred the conclusion of the Boston Marathon in 2013, expressions of courage and resilience spontaneously appeared. In a corner of Copley Square, just a stone's throw from the site of the explosions, people contributed hundreds of running shoes, pennants and personal notes to form a moving tribute to those who had suffered the most and express the city's stern resolve to face the future with confidence. The slogan "Boston Strong" cropped up everywhere, on storefronts, banners and tee-shirts. And there was even a flag bearing the words, "New York City loves Boston," a touching reminder that suffering can reduce the differences between arch rivals to insignificance.

Our instinctive refusal to succumb to suffering may explain why many people respond to a great loss by taking some sort of positive action. People often write books about their darkest experiences or take their story to the airwaves or the internet. At the very least, an account of what they have endured memorializes the experience. It is a way of saying, "It matters" or "I matter." They may also hope that those who face similar challenges will take comfort with the thought that they are not entirely alone.

People also respond to suffering by trying to help others avoid what they have been through. When I was a youngster, my friends and I took turns one day swinging back and forth on a long vine that was hanging from a tree in our front yard. It was a lot of fun until Jason slipped off and broke his leg. Before they took him to the hospital, Jason handed his pocketknife to one of the neighborhood men who cut the vine down so no one else would get hurt.

The greater the loss, it seems, the greater the desire people have to do something constructive. This is often true of the experience of people whose children die under tragic circumstances. Candy Lightner's teenage daughter was killed by a drunk driver while walking home with a friend one day. She responded by founding MADD, Mothers Against Drunk Driving. The influential organization calls for stronger laws against drunk driving and seeks to educate people, especially young people, about the dangers of drinking and driving. John Walsh's son was abducted from a shopping center in broad daylight. In the frantic aftermath, Walsh discovered that the communication among the law-enforcement agencies he asked for help was very ineffective. After his son's death, he founded the Adam Walsh Child Resource Center and served on the board of directors of the National Center for Missing & Exploited Children.

Amy Biehl was a Stanford University graduate, a Fulbright scholar and a world-class diver who went to South Africa to work among impoverished victims of apartheid. She was stabbed to death in 1993 by one of the very young men she had gone to help. Her parents decided to show that she had not died in vain. From then on, Peter and Linda Biehl divided their time between their home in Newport Beach, California and the township in South Africa where Amy had lived and died. They set up the Amy Biehl Foundation and used a lot of their own money to develop the kind of projects that Amy was interested in—tutoring programs for school children and businesses such as a bakery and a brick factory. The Biehls memorialized their daughter by committing themselves to her goals and continuing her work.[4]

In 2002 *Wall Street Journal* reporter Daniel Pearl was murdered by terrorists in Pakistan. Just before he died, he was videotaped

---

[4]Sandy Banks, "Out of Tragedy, a Legacy of Forgiveness," *Los Angeles Times*, April 9, 2002.

saying the words, "My father is Jewish, my mother is Jewish, I am Jewish." Two years later his father and mother published a book in his memory. Entitled *I Am Jewish: Personal Reflections Inspired by the Last Words of Daniel Pearl*, it contains the thoughts of 150 people on what it means to be a Jew. His parents also established the Daniel Pearl Foundation, which provides fellowships to journalists from parts of the world where anti-Semitism is widespread.[5]

While we can never undo the consequences of great suffering, we instinctively seek ways to respond to it resourcefully and creatively. People are determined to bring meaning to their suffering.

THE PHILOSOPHICAL BACKSTORY TO SOUL MAKING THEODICY

The idea that suffering serves a positive purpose, that its goal is to help us reach moral and spiritual maturity, has been around a long time. As we have seen, it is a familiar theme in the Bible. And it figures prominently in many books designed to help people cope with life's serious challenges—a serious illness, the death of a loved one, the end of a marriage or some other traumatic experience. For example, in his book *Where Is God When It Hurts?* bestselling author Philip Yancey labels pain "the gift nobody wants," and goes on to describe the many positive things that difficulties contribute to our lives.[6]

On a philosophical level, no one has developed this perspective on suffering more extensively than John Hick, an influential philosopher of religion. In fact, he is the one responsible for the widespread use of the expression "soul making." Although the world we live in is filled with suffering, Hick asserts, we shouldn't think of this as something necessarily negative. To the contrary, a world that contains suffering

---

[5]Patricia Ward Biederman, "New Book Explores the Meaning of Being Jewish," *Los Angeles Times,* March 6, 2004.
[6]Philip Yancey, *Where Is God When It Hurts?* (Grand Rapids: Zondervan, 1990), p. 25.

is the ideal environment for character development. For Hick, the goal of our existence is not to bask in comfort and pleasure, but to become mature, well-developed moral beings, and there is no way to achieve this without undergoing hardship and difficulty.

As every bodybuilder knows, it takes resistance for our muscles to grow. Similarly, the argument goes, it takes resistance for our souls to grow. Only by meeting challenges and over-coming obstacles can we develop positive traits of character. It's not hard to think of virtues that depend on the presence of suf-fering in some form. Compassion is an obvious example. If no one ever suffered there would be no opportunity to show com-passion, nor any need for it. Another example is courage. Courage presupposes danger. If we lived in a risk-free world, we could never become courageous. Similarly, patience, determi-nation, persistence—whatever you call it—could never develop in a world where everything came easily to us. We could go on, but the point is clear. The world we now live in, with all its perils and pitfalls, seems to provide just the sort of environment we need in order to develop spiritual and moral maturity.

Hick finds a precedent for his theodicy in the writings of a second-century church father, Irenaeus of Lyons.[7] Unlike Au-gustine, who believed that human beings were originally perfect, Irenaeus maintained that perfection was the end, not the beginning, of human existence. When their lives began, human beings were imperfect and immature. To reach perfection they needed to undergo a long period of development, and suffering would play an integral role in this process. Children do a lot of falling when they are learning to walk—that's why we call them "toddlers." Just as falling and getting up are a natural part of physical growth, experiencing

---

[7]John Hick, *Evil and the God of Love*, rev. ed. (New York: Harper & Row, 1978), pp. 211-15.

difficulties and setbacks, making mistakes and learning from them, forms a natural part of spiritual growth.

Hick's soul making theodicy resembles perfect plan theodicy in some respects and the free will defense in others. Like the perfect plan, soul making views suffering as part of God's overall design for the world. Suffering is not incomprehensible. It is not a gaping black hole in the framework of life. It plays an important role in the scheme of things.

Both soul making and free will theodicies affirm that human beings are free, but there is a significant difference between them. For the free will defense, in its classic expression, God wanted the creatures to *remain* loyal to God. But for soul making theodicy, God wanted the creatures to *become* loyal to God. When God decided to give some of the creatures significant personal freedom, God knew that they would make mistakes and suffer a host of painful consequences. But God also knew that they could learn from those mistakes, and God intended that they would eventually come to know and return God's love and embrace God's purposes for their lives.

The fact that God endowed the creatures with freedom, knowing they would make mistakes as a result, does not mean that God approves of their mistakes. Though God knew that the world would contain suffering, it doesn't follow that God wanted things to get as bad as they are. Nor does it mean that God is behind every instance of suffering that comes to us. But in deciding to give human beings genuine freedom, God made the commitment to respect our choices, even when they lead to consequences that are disastrous.

For these reasons, soul making theodicy is different in important ways from both perfect plan and free will responses to suffering. On the one hand, it gives suffering a place in the scheme of things that proponents of the free will defense often deny it. It sees suffering as a natural concomitant of freedom. On the other hand, unlike perfect plan theodicy, the soul making view does not see God's will behind every instance of suffering. If we ask whether soul making places suffering inside or outside God's will, the answer seems to be both. It is God's will that humans be free and learn from the suffering that freedom inevitably leads to. But God does not will all the suffering that flows from our mistakes.

QUESTIONS ABOUT SOUL MAKING THEODICY

Like every perspective on suffering, this theodicy raises several questions. The first is whether or not the soul making process reaches its objectives. If the purpose of suffering in the world is to perfect our characters, we might ask, where are the perfect characters? Does anyone in our world ever actually reach moral and spiritual perfection? It doesn't seem so, even on casual inspection. Once in a while a Mother Teresa appears, a person who vividly embodies lofty moral ideals. But such people are exceedingly rare. The vast majority of human lives, even those that span many decades, never come close to perfection.

Another question for soul making theodicy is whether or not the benefits that come from suffering are worth the price. In other words, is the soul making program cost effective? Even if suffering produces moral and spiritual improvements, it is hard to imagine that they justify the massive amount of suffering in the world.

This is particularly true in the case of what some philosophers call "horrendous evils." Many of life's challenges and inconveniences lead to benefits that far outweigh their cost. The disappointment I felt on not getting a job I was promised was more than made up for by the opportunity I then had to go on to something that was better for me. People who exercise vigorously often wind up with sore muscles. But getting in shape is worth the discomfort.

Medical students occasionally complain about all the information they are expected to master. But for most physicians, the rewards of the profession make up for the struggles of their training.

Other instances of suffering, however, refuse to fit this pattern. Some forms of suffering are so excruciating, and some are so massive, that they defy all attempts to find in them some beneficial purpose. Severely abused children are frequently damaged for life. Nothing that happens later on, overcomes, let alone compensates, for the trauma they endure. Thousands of American veterans returning from wars in the Middle East now suffer from PTSD and will never fully recover. And what benefits could possibly offset, or render even slightly acceptable, the unthinkable horrors of systematic torture, deliberate mutilation and genocide? Surely the Holocaust resists all explanation. How could anything ever make it comprehensible?

John Hick has an imaginative response to the observation that soul making does not seem to be working. He admits that very few admirable souls have emerged in human history. So he includes two additional elements in his theodicy. First, he suggests that the soul making begun in one's life on this earth is just the beginning of a long process. This life is merely the first in a series of lives to be lived in various places in the cosmos. So we will continue to undergo spiritual development on into the future, each of us at a rate appropriate to our distinctive needs and possibilities. Quite naturally, it will take some souls a great deal longer than others to reach maturity.

Second, Hick maintains, after a succession of lifespans and constant maturation, every soul will reach its ultimate destiny, namely, union with the divine, with God or "the Real," as he variously terms it. Sooner or later, in other words, every soul will achieve "salvation." If the notion of soul making makes any sense, he argues, the process must be effective, and if the process is truly effective, then it must be effective for everyone. Accordingly, in Hick's theodicy, every single person will eventually enjoy ultimate spiritual fulfillment. If indeed, ultimate reality consists of infinite love, then everyone will ultimately yield to its embrace. As Hick describes it, then, universal salvation is a necessary corollary of soul making theodicy.[8]

When it comes to "horrendous evils," other thinkers take an approach that bears some resemblance to Hick's. We may not be able to conceive or imagine how such sufferings could contribute to the fulfillment of any positive purpose, now or ever. But even so, we can still be confident that God's resources of love and benevolence are so vast that they can bring from these evils a positive contribution to our experience. God's love overcomes the evils of this world. It guarantees that our sufferings, even—or especially— the most horrific of them, will eventually prove to benefit us sometime in the course of our existence (if not in this life, then in the life to come) in ways we cannot now comprehend. We may not be able to explain just *how* it happens, but we can nevertheless affirm *that* it is so.

What Eleonore Stump refers to as the "mothering principle" may help us to understand this concept. Stump observes that a good mother might allow a child to suffer, but she would do so on two conditions only: that the benefits will ultimately outweigh the pain and that there is no other way to achieve those benefits. Since according to faith God loves us far more than our human parents do, and since God obviously allows us to suffer, we must conclude that God in infinite wisdom knows that we will ultimately benefit from our sufferings and that we could not enjoy these benefits in the

---

[8]Hick develops his ideas of ultimate human destiny in *Death and Eternal Life* (Louisville, KY: Westminster John Knox, 1994).

absence of suffering. Our trust in God's love and wisdom makes us confident that this is so.[9]

Marilyn McCord Adams makes a similar proposal in her discussion of "horrendous evils and the goodness of God."[10] She defines horrendous evils as those which threaten to "engulf" all the goodness in a person's life and leave the person believing that her life is not worth living. It is possible, Adams suggests, that victims of horror nevertheless experience the goodness of God, and they do so in such a way that the unique value of that experience is inextricably connected to what they are going through. How could this happen? "By integrating participation in horrendous evils into a person's relationship with God."[11] This could involve several things, including an awareness of God's own suffering and face-to-face communion with God after death. But the result is that sufferers would not choose to avoid the horrors they endure if that meant losing that particular manifestation of God's goodness. Thus, if horrendous evils are linked in significant ways to an intimate experience of God's presence, Adams argues, they are not only "engulfed" but "defeated" by good. For, "no one will wish away any intimate encounters with God from his/her life-history in this world."[12] Like Stump's mothering principle, Adams's view expresses profound confidence in the goodness and love of God. And like

---

[9]Eleonore Stump, personal communication, 2000.

[10]This is the title of both an article and a book. The article appears in *The Problem of Evil*, ed. Marilyn McCord Adams and Robert Merrihew Adams (New York: Oxford University Press, 1990), pp. 209-21; Marilyn McCord Adams, *Horrendous Evils and the Goodness of God* (Ithaca, NY: Cornell University Press, 1999).

[11]Adams, "Horrendous Evils," p. 218.

[12]Ibid., p. 219. Compare this statement in her book: "Everyone will eventually be enabled to recognize any antemortem participation in horrors as other moments of intimacy with God and so integrate them into the relationship that floods their lives with objective and (by then) recognized and appropriated positive meaning." The sufferings of this present life are thus concretely balanced off in beatific intimacy with God (Adams, *Horrendous Evils*, p. 162).

Hick's soul making theodicy, her view embraces a strong belief in the reality of a future beyond death. Indeed, it depends on a robust doctrine of personal immortality, and this, of course, raises questions of its own for many people.

Is there anything in personal experience now that supports the logic of Adams's position—anything that suggests that goodness can somehow engulf and defeat an experience on the order of a horrendous evil? Perhaps. A friend of mine died some time ago after a long, difficult yet valiant struggle with cancer. Once, sometime after it was over, his wife told me that his final pain-filled months had brought them closer to each other than they had ever been before. Together in suffering, she said emphatically, they experienced the most profound intimacy of their entire marriage. Perhaps God is uniquely near to us when we suffer horrendously, and the value of that closeness outweighs the cost of our suffering. While this approach defers our full awareness of this value to the life to come, it is a thought that brings comfort and courage to many people. As we anticipate developing a theodicy of our own, it will be helpful to keep in mind the emphasis that the soul making approach places on a strong and abiding confidence in God's infinite love and resourcefulness.

5

AN ENEMY HATH DONE THIS

Cosmic Conflict Theodicy

ONE OF MY FAVORITE COLLEGE TEACHERS was a professor of biblical studies. As a ministerial student I took a number of classes from him, more, actually, than from any anyone else on the faculty. He taught Greek and Hebrew and a number of other courses that required a knowledge of these languages. My professor loved the topics he was teaching, he was a good communicator, he enjoyed being with students, he had a great sense of humor. Perhaps most important, he was an excellent scholar. During the years I was his student he pursued his doctorate and completed all the requirements except the dissertation.

A couple of years after I graduated, I heard that this professor was having some health problems. And though he was a private person, the diagnosis soon became known. He had multiple sclerosis. I lived not far away, and the school asked me to cover one of his classes for a few weeks while he decided what to do. He managed to return to the classroom and teach from a wheelchair for a couple of years, but the progress of the disease eventually made that impossible. He took a medical retirement and lived in the community, where his family looked after him for a long time afterward. One day during a visit from the church pastor, he reflected on his predicament. "Every war has casualties," the professor observed. "There's a great war going on in the universe between good and evil, and I am one of the casualties of this conflict."

Another influential theodicy rests on the idea that human beings are involved in a conflict between superhuman forces of good and evil. At the center of this conflict stands the towering figure of God's archenemy, one being more than any other who is responsible for all that is wrong and painful in the world God created. This figure appears here and there in a number of biblical passages. One well known example is the prologue to the book of Job (Job 1–2). The Lord gave a figure named Satan permission to test Job. Subsequently, the man lost his possessions and his children and suffered severe physical affliction, yet remained faithful to God through it all. Then follows a long series of speeches by Job's friends, Job himself and finally God, speaking from a whirlwind, all presenting various perspectives on Job's predicament.[1]

The devil appears as Jesus' great adversary in the Gospels, tempting him in the wilderness, for example (Mt 4:1-11; Lk 4:1-13). The letter of 1 Peter warns its readers, "Like a roaring lion your adversary the devil prowls around, looking for someone to devour" (1 Pet 5:8). In a similar vein, Paul's letter to the Ephesians encourages Christians to "put on the whole armor of God," since they struggle against "the cosmic powers of this present darkness" and "the spiritual forces of evil in the heavenly places" (Eph 6:12-13). Superhuman conflict is nowhere more vividly portrayed than in the book of Reve-

---

[1]According to the standard interpretation of Job, the figure of Satan vanishes after the first two chapters of the book, leaving the man wondering why God has afflicted him so grievously. Some interpreters, however, find veiled references to a powerful opponent to God in later passages, such as Job 41 with its dramatic description of "Leviathan."

lation: "And war broke out in heaven; Michael and his angels fought against the dragon. The dragon and his angels fought back, but they were defeated, and there was no longer any place for them in heaven" (Rev 12:7-8). And later in Revelation the dragon is also identified as "that ancient serpent, who is the Devil and Satan" (Rev 20:2).

For many who suffer, as for my esteemed professor, the idea of a cosmic conflict is personally helpful. They believe their suffering does not come to them from God, but from something utterly opposed to God. It is caused by a diabolical power that is doing everything it can to thwart God's will for us and make our lives miserable. So, instead of wondering why God sends or allows or intends to use their suffering, their response is to say, "An enemy has done this" (Mt 13:28) and put the blame on him.

Although familiar to readers of the Bible, the devil appears rather infrequently in scholarly discussions of evil. Alvin Plantinga[2] and, following him, Stephen T. Davis,[3] describe the figure of Satan, the fallen angel Lucifer, as a potential explanation for natural evil. (The expression *luciferous* is that of Stephen Davis.) But their descriptions of Lucifer's activity are rather brief and incidental to the overall positions they develop. There are others, however, for whom the figure of the devil is indispensable to an adequate approach to suffering. One is Gregory A. Boyd, whose "trinitarian warfare worldview" places responsibility for the sufferings of the world squarely on the devil.[4]

---

[2]Alvin Plantinga, *God, Freedom, and Evil* (New York: Harper & Row, 1974), p. 58.
[3]Stephen T. Davis, "Free Will and Evil," in *Encountering Evil: Live Options in Theodicy*, ed. Stephen T. Davis (Louisville, KY: John Knox Press, 1981), pp. 74-75.
[4]Gregory A. Boyd, *God at War: The Bible and Spiritual Conflict* (Downers Grove, IL: InterVarsity Press, 1997); Gregory A. Boyd, *Satan and the Problem of Evil: Constructing a Trinitarian Warfare Theodicy* (Downers Grove, IL: InterVarsity Press, 2001). The objective of both volumes, Boyd states, "is to explore the significance of the biblical portrait of Satan for a contemporary theodicy." The purpose of *God at War* is to show that the biblical writers held a warfare worldview. The purpose of *Satan and the Problem of Evil* is to show how the early church lost sight of the warfare worldview and then to demonstrate that it provides for a theodicy that is superior to all alternatives (*God at War*, pp. 22-23).

To the question, "Is God to blame?" Boyd responds with an emphatic no.[5] And the reason, as he explains in several different books, is that God has enemies, and these enemies have great power. So it is they who bear responsibility for the world's sorrows and woes. Satan and his cohort of once angelic, now demonic, followers are the forces behind the strife and bloodshed that riddle human history. And their interference with the processes of nature has transformed the world from the perfect home God intends it to be into an ominous and threatening environment, marked by pain, disease and death.[6]

Boyd draws a sharp distinction between the warfare worldview and the picture of God that has prevailed through most of Christian history. In the "classical-philosophical portrait," God is the one supreme power in the universe, whose sovereign will is perfectly fulfilled throughout creation.[7] This "divine blueprint view," the view that God is directly responsible for everything that happens, generates the "problem of evil" in its classic formulation: *If God is perfect in goodness and power, why does evil exist? Wouldn't a supremely good and powerful being want to prevent it?* And this in turn imposes a deeply troubling question on anyone who suffers. *Why does God want me to suffer? Just what is my suffering supposed to accomplish?*

According to Boyd, both questions—*why?* and *why me?*—dissolve when we replace the classic picture of the God-world relation with the warfare worldview. The pervasiveness of suffering was not bewildering to those who lived during the eras of biblical history,

---

[5]Gregory A. Boyd, *Is God to Blame? Beyond Pat Answers to the Problem of Suffering* (Downers Grove, IL: InterVarsity Press, 2003).

[6]Asserts Boyd, "There is no such thing as 'natural' evil. Nature in its present state, I believe, is not as the Creator created it to be. . . . When nature exhibits diabolical features that are not the result of human wills, it is the direct or indirect result of the influence of diabolic forces" (*Satan and the Problem*, p. 247).

[7]Boyd, *God at War*, p. 69.

nor to those in the centuries that directly followed. To the contrary, they were keenly aware of the presence of evil powers, and they attributed the ills of life to them, not to God. If the universe is populated by a host of beings opposed to God and bent on wreaking death and destruction, it is hardly surprising that we suffer; it would be surprising if we didn't.

From the perspective of cosmic conflict theodicy, then, we do not suffer because God wants us to—God's role is to relieve suffering.[8] We suffer because we live in a war zone. We suffer because God's enemies are active in the world, and we have made ourselves vulnerable to violence.[9] So it is futile to look for a specific reason or purpose for suffering.

The warfare worldview has another ramification. "When we accept the warfare worldview of Scripture," Boyd says, "the intellectual problem of evil is transformed into the practical problem of evil."[10] Freed from the burden of explaining or comprehending suffering and empowered by the victory achieved by Jesus' death and resurrection, we are called to join in God's own work of resisting the forces of evil and devote ourselves to the work of relieving suffering. Jesus devoted his life to counteracting the forces of evil, to healing disease and casting out demons. If we follow in his footsteps, and in those of the earliest Christians, we too will enter the war against God's enemies. We too will confront and resist the forces of evil.[11]

---

[8]When they passed a man blind from birth, the disciples asked Jesus, "'Rabbi, who sinned, this man or his parents, that he was born blind?' Jesus answered, 'Neither this man nor his parents sinned; he was born blind so that God's works might be revealed in him'" (Jn 9:1-3).

[9]"By our own rebellion, we are caught in the crossfire of a cosmic war, and we suffer accordingly" (Boyd, *Is God to Blame?* p. 105).

[10]Boyd, *God at War,* p. 291.

[11]See the final chapter of Boyd's *God at War,* "Engaging the Powers: The Christian Life as Spiritual Warfare" (pp. 269-93).

Boyd is not alone among Christian thinkers to give the devil a prominent role in his account of suffering. Another is Ellen G. White, a prolific writer who lived in the nineteenth and early twentieth centuries.[12] In Boyd's estimation, she "integrated a warfare perspective into the problem of evil and the doctrine of God perhaps more thoroughly than anyone else in church history."[13] The central theme of Ellen White's theology appears in the title of her most influential book, *The Great Controversy Between Christ and Satan*. According to the preface, its purpose in part was "to present a satisfactory solution of the great problem of evil."[14]

Like Boyd, White places human suffering within the framework of a cosmic conflict. The conflict began with a revolt against God on the highest level of created beings, and it will end when God's enemies perish and God's loving purposes for creation are finally fulfilled. From this perspective, the devil is the source of all the world's ills, and everything that makes human life miserable is ultimately attributable to our participation in his rebellion against God.

White paints God's archenemy in decidedly Miltonian hues. Like the great antagonist in *Paradise Lost*, her Lucifer is a majestic figure, a covering cherub and head of the angelic host. Given his lofty position and great intelligence, he had deep insight into the nature of God. Yet at some point in time, Lucifer mysteriously, inexplicably came to resent God's authority. He aroused the suspicions of his fellow angels, portraying God as a tyrant unworthy of

---

[12]Best known as one of the founders of the Seventh-day Adventist Church, Ellen G. White's place in American religious history has received increasing attention in recent years. See, for example, Ann Taves, *Fits, Trances, and Visions: Experiencing Religion and Explaining Experience from Wesley to James* (Princeton, NJ: Princeton University Press, 1999), pp. 153-65.

[13]Boyd, *God at War*, p. 307n44.

[14]Ellen G. White, *The Great Controversy Between Christ and Satan* (1888; repr., Mountain View, CA: Pacific Press, 1950), p. xii. This is the final book in a five-volume series titled *Conflict of the Ages*.

their loyalty. Eventually he gained the sympathy of one-third of the heavenly host, and when their opposition ripened into open revolt, they were cast out of heaven.

With this expulsion, the central stage in this cosmic drama shifted to this earth, where Lucifer, now variously referred to as Satan and the devil, sought to spread his rebellion. When Adam and Eve ate from the forbidden tree, their disloyalty to God left them vulnerable to God's enemies, and ever since Satan and his angels have been busy wreaking havoc on the earth. These sinister forces are ultimately responsible for everything that threatens human life and well-being, from natural disasters and organic diseases to personal sin in all its manifestations—pride, self-indulgence, cruelty, crime and war. Beneath the veneer of human activity, the essence of history consists in the conflict between God and Satan as these great powers pursue their contrasting objectives for the earth, each attempting to counteract and undermine the work of the other.

As White describes it, the central issue in the great controversy is the character of God or, more precisely, the creaturely perception of God. Lucifer's persistent charge is that God is tyrannical and abusive, unworthy of creaturely devotion. To resolve the conflict, God needs to do more than defeat evildoers; God must do so in a way that would be perceived as fully consistent with love. And this is what the plan of salvation accomplished. It provided the definitive revelation of God's character. The gift of God's own Son to live a life of suffering service vividly displays God's love and exposes the emptiness of Satan's accusations. It is really *his* dominion that rests on cruelty and tyranny, not God's. The cross was the turning point in the great controversy, and it benefits the entire universe. With Christ's death, "the last link of sympathy between Satan and the heavenly world was broken." So "all heaven triumphed in the Saviour's victory. Satan was defeated, and knew that his kingdom was lost."[15]

The controversy will continue until the end of time, revealing that the devil's charges against God's character are utterly without foundation. And when evil is finally eradicated from the universe the "terrible experiment of rebellion" will serve as "a perpetual safeguard to all holy intelligences, to prevent them from being deceived as to the nature of transgression."[16] The universe will therefore be secure from all further rebellion. "A tested and proved creation will never again be turned from allegiance to Him whose character has been fully manifested before them as fathomless love and infinite wisdom."[17]

Ellen White's theodicy takes the form of an extended narrative, rather than a theological or philosophical discourse like Boyd's, but their ideas share certain features with free will theodicy. Both attribute the origin of evil to the exercise of creaturely freedom. Because God is a God of love, God desires that the creatures serve God out of love, and they can do this only if they are genuinely free.[18] Giving the creatures freedom carried a risk, however—they could choose to reject rather than return God's love. But even though this is what happened, there is nothing in freedom as such that logically leads to sin. Lucifer's rebellion was inexplicable and incomprehensible. Sin is "an intruder," White

---

[15]Ellen G. White, *The Desire of Ages* (1898; repr., Mountain View, CA: Pacific Press, 1940), pp. 758, 762.

[16]White, *Great Controversy*, p. 499.

[17]Ibid., p. 504.

[18]"God desires from all His creatures the service of love—homage that springs from an intelligent appreciation of His character. He takes no pleasure in a forced allegiance, and to all He grants freedom of will" (White, *Great Controversy*, p. 493). Love "must be freely chosen," insists Boyd. "It cannot be coerced. Agents must possess the capacity and opportunity to reject love if they are to possess the genuine capacity and opportunity to engage in love" (Boyd, *Satan and the Problem*, p. 52).

asserts, "for whose presence no reason can be given. It is mysterious, unaccountable."[19]

There are also elements in Boyd's and White's accounts that resemble soul making theodicy. Though the fall was not what God originally intended, White maintains, it resulted in an environment that was beneficial to moral growth. After human beings yielded to temptation, they needed the discipline that only hardship could provide.[20] Similarly, Boyd argues that no matter what happens to us, God can turn it to our advantage. God may not be the cause of suffering, but God "wisely uses suffering to build our character and strengthen our reliance on him. While we need not assume there is a divine purpose *leading to* our suffering, we can and must trust that there is a divine purpose that *follows from it*."[21] Filled with sorrows though it is, this world is potentially a "vale of soul-making."[22]

QUESTIONS ABOUT COSMIC CONFLICT THEODICY

No theodicy is more dramatic than that of cosmic conflict, spotlighting as it does the fascinating, enigmatic figure of Lucifer, the archangel who became God's archenemy. As with other theodicies, however, this approach to evil also raises some perplexing questions. One concerns its basic plausibility. Is there indeed a cosmic conflict raging all around us? Are we surrounded by invisible personalities? Do superhuman powers actually influence the course of nature and history?

---

[19]White, *Great Controversy*, p. 493; cf. p. 503: "In the final execution of the judgment it will be seen that no cause for sin exists."

[20]Ibid., pp. 60-61. A "life of toil and care" was "part of God's great plan for man's recovery from the ruin and degradation of sin."

[21]Boyd, *Is God to Blame?* p. 196, italics original.

[22]This well-known expression first appeared in one of the letters of the English poet John Keats. "Call the world if you please 'The vale of Soul-Making.'" (Letter to George and Georgiana Keats, April 21, 1819, in *Letters of John Keats 1814-1821*, ed. H. E. Rollins [Cambridge, MA: Harvard University Press, 2002]).

Such a view of things seems to fly in the face of our modern perspective. Today people instinctively look to science and technology for an understanding of the world we live in. We turn to meteorologists to explain hurricanes, geologists to account for earthquakes and physicians to ascertain the causes of disease. We may affirm God as the ultimate cause and designer of the world, but we do not typically invoke divine activity as a way of accounting for specific physical phenomena. And though we may affirm divine providence, we do not characteristically assert that God directly caused specific historical events. People seldom appeal to angels, demons or other invisible personalities to account for things that happen.

Perhaps this is why most philosophical treatments of evil today do without the devil. In his extensive writings on theodicy John Hick makes no use of the idea of a prehuman angelic fall or the notion that the world is in the grip of demonic powers.[23] And even though she addresses "horrendous evils," which she calls "the deepest of religious problems," Marilyn McCord Adams does not consider the figure of the devil. The index to her book on that topic contains no references to "devil," "Lucifer" or "Satan."[24]

Along with this general reservation, there are elements in the views of Boyd and White that seem problematic. One is the very concept of cosmic conflict. The idea of a superhuman agent whose revolt engulfs the entire universe and poses a genuine threat to God's government seems incoherent in light of traditional concepts of divine power and sovereignty. How could any created being pose a serious challenge to God? After all, as Creator, God not only brought the universe into being, it is God's power that sustains all

---

[23]John Hick, *Evil and the God of Love*, rev. ed. (New York: Harper & Row, 1978), p. 333.
[24]Marilyn McCord Adams, "Horrendous Evils and the Goodness of God," in *The Problem of Evil* (New York: Oxford University Press, 1990), p. 211. The devil is also absent from her later book by the same title, *Horrendous Evils and the Goodness of God* (Ithaca, NY: Cornell University Press, 1999).

that exists, moment by moment.[25] But if everything owes its existence to God, how could any created being, even the most highly exalted, pose a plausible threat to God? What would intelligent beings hope to gain from contesting God's supremacy, if they knew that God could instantly annihilate them?

Another question concerns the idea of "God on trial." As Ellen White describes it, the central issue of the great controversy is whether God *deserves* the loyalty of the creatures, or to be precise, whether they *believe* that God deserves their loyalty.[26] The devil fomented doubt about God. He accused God of being overbearing, tyrannical, and not at all benevolent or loving. Over the long course of human history, sufficient evidence accumulates to demonstrate conclusively the truth about God's character, and eventually all God's creatures will acknowledge that God is a being of "pure, unbounded love"—exactly what God has always claimed to be. When God's true nature is fully realized, the central issue of the conflict is settled, the devil loses his argument, and the controversy is effectively over—case closed.

But there is something odd about the notion of weighing evidence when it comes to God. How could God be the object of impartial inquiry? To come to reliable conclusions of any sort, we must be confident that we are looking at evidence that has not been tampered with and that our minds are functioning reliably. Given God's unique status in the universe, however, nothing in the way of evidence exists unless God's power sustains it, and our minds work the way they do because God designed them that way. As a result, every

---

[25]Paul's quotation of a pagan poet is often cited in this connection: "In him we live and move and have our being" (Acts 17:28).

[26]What is really at stake, to put it another way, is not God's power, but God's reputation. For a scholarly examination of God's reputation in the context of the biblical book of Revelation, see Sigve K. Tonstad, *Saving God's Reputation: The Theological Function of Pistis Iesou in the Cosmic Narratives of Revelation* (New York: T & T Clark, 2006).

claim to know something implicitly presupposes that God has neither tampered with the evidence nor manipulated our thinking. To determine *if* God is trustworthy, therefore, we must assume *that* God is trustworthy. And this, in effect, begs the question.

There are features of Boyd's account that seem problematic too. Besides an overall sketch of supernatural forces in conflict, he describes the way these forces operate in certain situations. Prayer, he says, for example, "is fundamentally a *warfare activity,*"[27] and "God's will is often thwarted by evil cosmic forces."[28] Among a number of variables related to prayer, he lists "angelic free will" and "the strength and number of spirit agents." Because "things in the spiritual realm are not dissimilar to things in the physical realm," what transpires in response to a specific prayer may be determined by "the strength and number of angels fighting on one side or the other."[29] Although there are certain biblical statements that contain such allusions—Boyd frequently cites Daniel 10:12-13, which describes an angel's delay in responding to Daniel's prayer—the idea that the answer to a prayer could be determined by the outcome of a skirmish between invisible personalities will strike many as imaginative, but not particularly helpful on a personal religious level.

THE ENDURING ATTRACTION OF COSMIC CONFLICT THEODICY

In spite of its limited philosophical influence, many people find the idea of cosmic conflict plausible and personally helpful. As Boyd observes, secularism, with its dismissal of the supernatural, is no longer as influential as it once was. We have seen a "postmodern awakening" in the past few decades in which the "narrow struc-

---

[27]Boyd, *Satan and the Problem,* p. 235.
[28]Boyd, *God at War,* p. 291.
[29]Boyd, *Is God to Blame?* p. 143.

tures of modern Western naturalistic categories" are becoming increasingly irrelevant, and people are less willing to dismiss the perspectives of other historical eras and other cultures today as implausible, "primitive" or "superstitious."[30]

On a popular level, of course, the supernatural has never lost its attraction, and if anything it seems to have increased in recent years. Angels have been featured in national news magazines, major motion pictures and a network television series. And millions of people are intrigued by the devil. He is a familiar character in movies and novels. He figures prominently in a wide range of religious phenomena, evoking responses that range from fear, revulsion and defiance to admiration and even worship, and he has even made an appearance in popular psychology.[31]

There is another factor that gives the superhuman personification of evil plausibility. Certain forms of suffering are of such duration, intensity or magnitude that they defy comprehension. Only a cause of superhuman, indeed, near-cosmic proportions, it seems, could possibly account for them. The Holocaust made the idea of the devil plausible for many in the twentieth century.[32] For more recent examples, we have only to think of the thousands who perished on September 11, 2001, ethnic cleansing in the former Yugoslavia, the massacre of millions in Rwanda, Democratic Republic of the Congo and other African countries, and the continuing bloodshed in the Middle East. Coming closer to home, we can all recall instances of cruelty and violence so outrageous, so

---

[30]Boyd, *God at War*, pp. 61-63.

[31]See M. Scott Peck, *People of the Lie: The Hope for Healing Human Evil* (New York: Simon & Schuster, 1983).

[32]In *God at War*, Boyd tells the appalling story of a Jewish girl in the Warsaw ghetto whose beautiful eyes were plucked out by two Nazi soldiers (pp. 33-34). Such radical, concrete evil resists attempts to place it within some abstract category, rendering it logically comprehensible. Instead, Boyd argues, it demands concrete resistance, not rational explanation.

beyond what humans alone could conceive, that they cry out for some cosmic explanation. They become remotely comprehensible only when attributed to a superhuman, supernatural, demonic source.

It seems natural to speak of suffering on a grand scale with language freighted with cosmic connotations. Ever since 9/11 people as prominent as the President of the United States have described international terrorism as "evil." And the idea that superhuman forces lie behind great moral conflicts speaks to us at a deeply intuitive level, as popular movies such as *The Lord of the Rings* series and *Man of Steel* indicate. Behind the spectacles that entertain us lies a specter that haunts us.

There is another reason to ponder cosmic conflict carefully, and that is the notion of divine deliverance it conveys. For this theodicy, God is no detached executive, serenely presiding over the cosmos, like a CEO in the corner suite of a high-rise office building, far removed from the rough and tumble of the streets below. To the contrary, God is a powerful force within the world, challenging and resisting the agents of evil at every turn. This picture of God can be greatly reassuring to people who feel helpless before the forces arrayed against them. There are those whose losses and failures leave them feeling utterly defeated, their lives devoid of meaning. There are people in the throes of enslaving habits, such as serious addictions, that have so exhausted their energies and depleted their resolve that nothing in the sphere of natural remedies or conventional treatment can help. When recovery programs, self-help regimens and medications all fail, people may feel that they are in the grip of an enemy possessing supernatural strength. And for them the idea of divine victory and divine deliverance may provide them their only basis for hope. The assurance that we are connected to a power mightier than any of its foes, and any of our foes, can be an immense source of comfort and strength. So the notion of cosmic conflict, with its assurance that God can defeat all that harms and threatens us and will eventually eradicate suffering entirely, can play an important role in a practical theodicy.

As soul making and cosmic conflict theodicies reveal, the notion that suffering lies outside God's will can lead to varying conclusions. There are thinkers whose embrace of creaturely freedom takes them in still other directions as they reflect on God's relation to suffering, as we shall see in the next two chapters.

6

LOVE MAKES THE WORLD GO ROUND

Openness of God Theodicy

As a prosecuting attorney in Los Angeles County, Vincent Bugliosi achieved convictions for members of the notorious Manson family back in the seventies. Later on he turned to writing, and in the epilogue to a book on the O. J. Simpson trial, Bugliosi lists a number of reasons explaining why he seriously doubts the existence of God. Predictably, the most basic reason he gives is the difficulty of accepting the idea that the world we live in was created by an absolute being who is perfect in power and goodness.

Something else that makes this belief hard for Bugliosi to accept is what he was taught years ago about divine fore-knowledge—the concept that God can see in advance the entire future, including the course of human history as a whole and the complete life story of every human being. While a student in parochial school, Bugliosi recalls, he asked the Monsignor who visited his classroom occasionally why God created certain people when he knew they were going to lead sinful lives and burn in hell for their actions. Why would God create future sinners? According to Bugliosi, the Monsignor didn't answer his question then, and he believes that no one ever has.[1]

The idea that God foresees future free decisions makes the problem of suffering particularly vexing because it gives God the perfect way to prevent it. If people suffer because some of them sin, and God knew in advance which ones would sin, why didn't God create only those beings that God foreknew would be loyal to God?

We have already considered one way of responding to this objection. According to perfect plan theodicy, everything happens just the way God designs it and it is all for the best. This does not mean that nothing is really evil. It means that even what we call evil, and what is ostensibly opposed to God's purposes, actually has an appropriate place in God's overall plan for the world. Once we understand the true purpose of creation, evil is no longer an obstacle to belief in God. All that happens serves the ultimate glory of God.

But there is another way of responding to Bugliosi's objection. Suppose we revise our concept of divine foreknowledge and with it our overall understanding of God's relation to the world. This is the approach of those who embrace a position known as "the openness of God," or "open theism."[2]

Central to open theism is the idea that God's relation to the creaturely world is highly interactive. God not only influences the world, the world also influences God. Consequently, events in

---

[1]Vincent Bugliosi, "God, Where Are You?" in *Outrage: The Five Reasons Why O. J. Simpson Got Away with Murder* (New York: Norton, 1996), pp. 334-35. Bugliosi amplifies the reservations mentioned in this epilogue to book length in a later publication, *Divinity of Doubt: The God Question* (New York: Vanguard, 2011).

[2]The best-known expression of open theism is Clark Pinnock et al., *The Openness of God: A Biblical Challenge to the Traditional Understanding of God* (Downers Grove, IL: InterVarsity Press, 1994). Others include Richard Rice, *God's Foreknowledge and Man's Free Will* (Minneapolis: Bethany House, 1985); Clark H. Pinnock, *Most Moved Mover: A Theology of God's Openness* (Grand Rapids: Baker Academic, 2001); and John Sanders, *The God Who Risks: A Theology of Divine Providence*, 2nd ed. (Downers Grove, IL: InterVarsity Press, 2007).

the creaturely world make a real difference to God . . . as they happen. According to traditional theology, God perceives the entire course of creaturely events in one timeless perception. Past, present and future are equally vivid to God. But for the open view of God, God's knowledge of the temporal world is also temporal. God experiences things as they happen, and God's knowledge of events develops as events take place.[3] God doesn't see the future in all its detail, because a great deal of the future is not there to be known.

This doesn't mean that the future is a complete blank as far as God is concerned. After all, a great deal that is going to happen is determined by what has already happened—an assumption that all of science depends on. So God knows everything that will happen as a direct result of what has already happened. In other words, God knows all the effects of present causes.[4] God also knows everything that *could* happen; in other words, God knows all possibilities. But something God doesn't know is the content of future free decisions. God doesn't know what our choices will be until we make them. Of course, God knows the range of possibilities available to us, and among these possibilities, which options we are more likely and which we are less likely to select. But the precise content of our choices is unknown, because it is unknowable, until we make them.

Openness theodicy has a lot in common with the free will defense, as we described it in chapter three. To relieve God of responsibility for suffering, it locates the origin of evil in the misuse of

---

[3]Gregory A. Boyd speaks of "the God who moves with us in time." *Satan and the Problem of Evil: Constructing a Trinitarian Warfare Theodicy* (Downers Grove, IL: InterVarsity Press, 2001), p. 100.

[4]To quote Clark H. Pinnock, one of the best known openness theologians, "According to openness theism . . . the future is partly settled and partly unsettled, partly determined and partly undetermined." (*Most Moved Mover*, p. 13).

creaturely freedom. But it differs from traditional versions of the free will defense by rejecting the notion of absolute foreknowledge. Openness theodicy insists that the future is genuinely open. Therefore the entrance of sin into the world, and the suffering it led to, were not inevitable. Things really could have taken a different direction.

The denial of absolute foreknowledge is just a facet of open theism, and not its most important feature. More basic is the idea that God is highly involved in the world. God cares about it. God responds to it. God can act within it. And God will ultimately redeem it. All this points to the central, most fundamental attribute of the divine character, namely, love. For open theology, as for various other theological perspectives, love is not just one among several divine qualities, it identifies the very nature of God.[5] God's very essence is to love ("God is love," 1 Jn 4:8). Indeed, God's innermost reality is a triune fellowship of love, and love characterizes all that God does—God's original decision to create and God's unconditional commitment to the objects of divine creation, to the world and all its inhabitants.[6]

The opening chapter of the Bible paints a highly interactive picture of God's relation to the world. According to this description, God creates in perfect freedom. God creates because God chooses to do so, not because anything, external or internal, compels God to do so. Furthermore, God exercises complete control over the creative process. The world owes its existence entirely to divine activity, and it is fully responsive to God's creative power. God

---

[5]For John Sanders, as for John Wesley, love is the "preeminent characteristic of God." "Personhood, relationality and community—not power, independence and control—become the center for understanding the nature of God" (*God Who Risks*, p. 177).

[6]Thomas Jay Oord emphasizes the kenotic, or self-emptying, self-sacrificing quality of God's love in his exposition of open theism, *The Nature of Love: A Theology* (St. Louis: Chalice, 2010).

speaks and creation does God's bidding. Consequently, there is a radical distinction between God and the created world. They represent different orders of reality. The world is not divine; it is not an extension of the divine being. And while the world depends on God for its existence, God's existence does not depend on the world. The relation between God and the world is asymmetrical.[7]

While it sharply distinguishes God from the world, this portrayal of creation describes God as intimately connected to the world. For one thing, God's creation is a profound expression of God's identity. It is more than a product of divine power; it is a revelation of the divine character. It is more like a work of art than a mere artifact. So, even though the world is not identical to God nor necessary for God's existence, neither is the world merely incidental to God. The world obviously matters a great deal to God. God invests great thought in the forms and functions of its inhabitants. Repeatedly throughout Genesis 1, God pronounces the objects of creative activity "good" or "very good."

While the world depends on God for its existence, and serves as an expression of God's thoughts, it is not just an extension of God's own ideas. God might have determined the contents of the world down to the last detail, but God didn't. Instead, God gave the creatures their own work to do. God told them to be fruitful and multiply. God invited humans to exercise dominion. As a result, the world has its own integrity, and to a certain extent the world charts its own course. God's creatures have their own con-

---

[7]Open theism shares with process thought (see chap. 7) the concept of divine temporality and the vision of God-world interaction, but it differs from the latter by maintaining that, while the world contributes to God's concrete experience, God's very existence does not require the existence of a creaturely world. For open theism, as for classical theism, the existence of God is necessary; the existence of the world is not. For a discussion of the similarities and differences between process and open theism, see John B. Cobb Jr. and Clark H. Pinnock, eds., *Searching for an Adequate God: A Dialogue Between Process and Free Will Theists* (Grand Rapids: Eerdmans, 2000).

tribution to make. We might say that God left the future up to them. And what becomes of them depends in large measure on their own actions and decisions.

In creating a world that could cooperate with God, however, God created a world that could disappoint God. There are risks involved in creating beings who are themselves creative. They may use their freedom to resist God's will and thwart God's purposes.[8] Sadly, according to the biblical narrative, this is what happened. And the Bible records God's reaction. God was keenly disappointed, but did not give up on the world. God did not simply wipe it out and start over. Instead, God worked over time to mitigate the effects of sin and to pursue God's original objectives for creation.

So it is clear that God remains permanently committed to the world God created. When God gave human beings responsibility, or dominion, over creation, it was not because God was no longer interested in it, nor because God no longer intended to be involved in it. To the contrary, as God's sabbath rest signifies (Gen 2:1-3), God's embrace of the created world would continue, for better or worse, for all time to come. Consequently, God cares for the world even now, in spite of all that has gone wrong. God is deeply affected by it, and God is active in its ongoing life, constantly working to redeem and restore it. As God does so, however, God consistently works in ways that respect the decisions of the creatures. What God does, and what God can do, depends to a significant degree on what they do.

---

[8]As Terence Fretheim comments on Gen 6:6-7, which states that God was sorry that God had created humankind on the earth, "This text is a witness to divine vulnerability in the unfolding creation. This is a God who takes risks, who makes the divine self vulnerable to the twists and turns of creational life, including human resistance. . . . The resistibility of God's will becomes a key for understanding many biblical texts that follow." *Creation Untamed: The Bible, God, and Natural Disasters* (Grand Rapids: Baker Academic, 2010), pp. 58-59.

In the view of open theists, all of this supports their central claim that God's experience of the dynamic world is itself dynamic.[9] God maintains an intimate connection with the world and experiences its ongoing life in an ongoing way. It is important to explore the theological backstory for each theodicy, as we have done here in the case of open theism, because suffering raises global questions and an effective response to suffering requires global answers. It is even more important, however, for us to return from these cosmic issues and ask what each theodicy means for someone in the throes of suffering. Having looked at open theism, we will now take a look at openness theodicy.

SUFFERING AND THE OPENNESS OF GOD

When it comes to human suffering, the central feature of open theism, its interactive view of God, means that God is genuinely affected by everything we go through, good and bad.[10] God rejoices when we rejoice, sorrows when we sorrow. So there is nothing that happens to us that does not affect God. As Jesus said, God takes note when a sparrow falls, and counts the very the hairs of our head (Mt 10:29-30). For openness theodicy, then, we are never beyond the reach of God's love and care. Since God shares our experiences to the fullest, we know that God is with us in our suffering. Indeed, in a sense God may be closer to us when we are suffering than at any other time. As the psalmist says, "Even though I walk through the darkest valley, I fear no evil; for you are with me" (Ps 23:4).

---

[9]Fretheim identifies "relatedness" as "the root image for thinking about God in the Bible" (*Creation Untamed*, p. 131).

[10]For an extended discussion of the problem of suffering from the perspective of open theism, see William Hasker, *The Triumph of God over Evil: Theodicy for a World of Suffering*, Strategic Initiatives in Evangelical Theology (Downers Grove, IL: InterVarsity Press, 2008). Along with his works on cosmic conflict theodicy, Gregory A. Boyd addresses suffering from the openness perspective in *Is God to Blame? Beyond Pat Answers to the Problem of Suffering* (Downers Grove, IL: InterVarsity Press, 2003).

The cross of Christ has many things to teach us, but none is more vivid or important than the fact that God is fully acquainted with suffering. Indeed, God participates in it. God knows the meaning of physical and emotional distress. As the supreme expression of God's love in human history (Jn 3:16), Jesus reveals that God understands the pain of loss and loneliness, the bewildering, disorienting experience of abandonment and isolation. As Hebrews states in its description of Jesus' present priestly ministry, "We do not have a high priest who is unable to sympathize with our weaknesses, but we have one who in every respect has been tested as we are, yet without sin" (Heb 4:15). Because he too has suffered, and because he shares and bears our sorrows with us, we are never alone when we suffer.

Open theism also affirms that suffering is not part of God's will for us. The healing ministry of Jesus underscores the fact that God is on the side of life and health. God takes no pleasure in seeing God's children suffer. Consequently, we should never view God as the source of suffering. It is not something God wants for any of us. For open theism, this is not only true on the universal scale, it is also true on the personal scale. When we suffer, there is nothing to be gained by trying to find a specific divine purpose or reason for it.

At least twice during his ministry, Jesus had a perfect opportunity to explain why certain people were the victims of misfortune. One day he and his disciples passed a blind man and they asked him, "Rabbi, who sinned, this man or his parents, that he was born blind?" Jesus answered, "Neither this man nor his parents sinned; he was born blind so that God's works might be revealed in him" (Jn 9:1-3). On another occasion, "there were some present who told him about the Galileans whose blood Pilate had mingled with their sacrifices. He asked them, 'Do you think that because these Galileans suffered in this way they were worse sinners than all other

Galileans? No, I tell you; but unless you repent, you will all perish as they did'" (Lk 13:1-3).

On neither occasion did Jesus explain why misfortune befell the particular people involved, why it was they, rather than others, who suffered. Instead of asking what lay behind the suffering, Jesus directed his listeners' attention to what lay beyond the suffering. He shifted the focus from "Why this?" to "What now?" In the case of the man born blind, he emphasized God's ability to act for good. In the case of the murdered Galileans, he emphasized the importance of being spiritually prepared for anything that might befall us. There are things we can learn from suffering, but why it is that certain people suffer and others don't is not one of them. When suffering comes to us, therefore, there is nothing to be gained from asking "Why me?" We should never assume that our suffering is something that God intends for us.

While God is touched by our sufferings, open theists believe, God is not just a passive observer. God responds resourcefully and creatively to the things that happen to us and works for good in the midst of life's disappointments and setbacks. As the apostle Paul exclaims, "All things work together for good for those who love God, who are called according to his purpose" (Rom 8:28). This doesn't mean that everything is ultimately good. Nothing makes it good that bad things happen. What it means is that God works for good, no matter what happens. God doesn't let suffering have the last word. Instead, God responds to every situation in ways that promote growth and healing. God works to bring about something good, no matter how bad things may be.

For open theists, it is also important to remember that God always acts in ways that take into account the decisions of God's creatures. As a result, God does not prevent us from hurting each other. God may not miraculously intervene to spare our lives or prevent us from falling ill. If God lets the world be the world, as some theologians are fond of saying, then God must respect the consequences to which our actions lead. For actions to have real integrity, they must have real results. After all, freedom is more than making a decision, it also involves making a difference.

Open theism also embraces the hope for "new heavens and a new earth, where righteousness is at home" (2 Pet 3:13). Open theists look forward to a future when God will wipe away every tear, when death will be no more, when mourning and crying and pain will be no more (Rev 21:4). So, open theism shares the hope of traditional Christianity that God will bring about a cosmic transformation and usher in a new order of things.

Questions About Openness Theodicy

As we have seen, every attempt to respond to suffering raises questions, and openness theodicy is no exception. For many people, open theism presents a view of God that is far too limited. In particular, it seems to diminish both divine knowledge and divine power.[11] Unless God knows the future completely, they ask, how can God's knowledge be perfect? And unless God has complete control over the world, how can God be worthy of worship? Is it conceivable that the almighty God would create beings who really had the ability to resist God's will, thwart God's purposes and disrupt God's plans for the world?

---

[11]Cf. the following titles: R. K. McGregor Wright, *No Place for Sovereignty: What's Wrong with Freewill Theism* (Downers Grove, IL: InterVarsity Press, 1996); Bruce A. Ware, *God's Lesser Glory: The Diminished God of Open Theism* (Wheaton, IL: Crossway Books, 2000); and Douglas Wilson, *Bound Only Once: The Failure of Open Theism* (Moscow, ID: Canon Press, 2001). Recent discussions of divine foreknowledge include Millard J. Erickson, *What Does God Know and When Does He Know It? The Current Controversy over Divine Foreknowledge* (Grand Rapids: Zondervan, 2003); and Steven C. Roy, *How Much Does God Foreknow? A Comprehensive Biblical Study* (Downers Grove, IL: InterVarsity Press, 2006).

Open theists reply that a great deal depends on just how we define "omniscience." Perfect knowledge is best understood, they argue, not simply as "knowing everything," but as "knowing everything there is to know." So before we can decide whether God knows the future, we need to know if the future is entirely knowable, whether it is complete in all its detail. If it is, then of course, God knows it. But if it isn't, if parts of the future are still undecided, then God's not knowing them doesn't mean that God's knowledge is imperfect. It simply means that God knows things just as they are—God knows the possible as possible and the actual as actual. Consequently, God knows the future exactly as it is: as partly definite and partly indefinite. One open theist puts the point this way: "The open view of God . . . affirms that the future decisions of self-determining agents are only possibilities until agents freely actualize them. In this view . . . the future is partly comprised of possibilities. And since God knows all things perfectly . . . God knows the future as partly comprised of possibilities."[12]

For open theists, God took a genuine risk when God made beings who were significantly free. There was a real possibility that they would use their freedom to reject God's love and rebel. Now, was it irresponsible for God to take such risks when God created the world? It all depends. What were the potential consequences of creaturely rebellion? And how likely was the rebellion to occur? And, perhaps most important, what motivated God to run this risk?

If love is the most fundamental quality of God's character, then we should look to love to explain why God created and what sort of world God made. Creation brings to expression the love that

---

[12]Boyd, *Satan and the Problem*, pp. 90-91. Boyd embraces openness theodicy as well as cosmic conflict theodicy. In fact, he regards the open view of God, or as he prefers to identify it, the open view of the future, as fully compatible with cosmic conflict theodicy. Not all open theists, however, find the notion of cosmic conflict helpful.

God intrinsically is. Accordingly, God loves the world God created, and God created a world that could return God's love. God made creatures who could appreciate and respond to God's love for them. To do this, however, their love and loyalty had to be voluntary.[13]

This is the basic scenario that all who subscribe to the free will defense accept. For most of them, however, it is a foregone conclusion that freedom would ultimately issue in suffering. Sooner or later, they hold, it was inevitable that morally free beings, at least some of them, would rebel and suffer as a result. Moreover, most of those who accept the free will defense also believe that the consequences of rebelling are, shall we say, "manageable." Sin disturbs but does not dismantle God's purposes for the world. God puts the plan of salvation into effect, and this effectively meets the need.

For John Hick, the best known advocate of soul making theodicy, it was not only God's plan that creatures be free, but also that they would fall from grace and be restored. To put it succinctly, the fall was inevitable, but the consequences were ultimately beneficial. For Alvin Plantinga's free will defense, things are a bit different. The rebellion of moral beings was not only possible but likely, if not inevitable, and the consequences were perhaps moderate rather than minimal. For both, however, it is no surprise that freedom led to rebellion and suffering.

There may be another way of looking at the fall, however, and it fits nicely with the open view of God. Suppose we reverse the more familiar approach. Suppose the likelihood of rebellion was slight and the results were potentially catastrophic. What then? On this scenario, God did everything possible to minimize the chance that anyone would rebel. As described in Genesis 1-2, for example, God made elaborate provisions for human happiness and clearly explained

---

[13]Boyd is emphatic on this point. Love, he insists, "must be freely chosen. It cannot be coerced. Agents must possess the capacity and opportunity to reject love if they are to possess the genuine capacity and opportunity to engage in love" (*Satan and the Problem*, p. 52).

the consequences of rebellion ("You shall surely die"), hoping that these manifestations of love and care would win their lasting loyalty. They didn't, of course. But even so, it is conceivable that the likelihood of creaturely rebellion, though real, was nevertheless very slight.

On this scenario, the plan of salvation was just that—a plan, a plan to be implemented should the need arise, but not an integral part of God's original design for creation. When the terrible emergency arose, the plan went into effect, and the rest, as they say, is history. But the fact that God's saving activity met the need so effectively indicates not that the need was a foregone conclusion but that God was prepared for its possibility.

Is this account of things implausible? Perhaps, but that may be due to the fact that it is hard for us to imagine a world that is significantly different from the one we live in. After all, on the level of everyday events, we often have the feeling that what happens was meant to happen. So it is easy to suppose that sin and suffering could not have been avoided. On the other hand, as we look back on the torturous history of human life, it is certainly possible for us to wonder how different things could have been, had human beings followed God's original plan and sin had never occurred.

THE APPEAL OF OPEN THEISM

For some, the idea that God knows everything that is going to happen to them is immensely reassuring. But others find comfort in the thought that God does not know the details of our lives in advance. Years ago a seminary teacher I know told me about a student who came to see him. The young man was bewildered and discouraged. His wife had decided to leave him. She had come to realize that she did not want to be married to a minister after all, and she did not want to be married to him in particular. Adding to the pain of separation, he also felt a great deal of confusion. Before they got married, he said, he and his wife prayed earnestly for guidance in planning their future. They believed the Lord had answered their prayers and was leading them to join their lives and prepare to serve God together in ministry. So why had things gone so terribly wrong? He always believed that God sees the future, the student said, so God surely knew what was going to happen to their marriage at the very time they were asking God for guidance. But if God knew that, why didn't God prevent them from going ahead with their plans? Why didn't God warn them that they were not suited for life together? God could have spared them the pain they were going through.

The professor recommended a book on the open view of God. And after reading it, the student returned for another conversation. He was greatly relieved. What if the future was not, as he had thought, entirely clear to God? What if his wife changed her mind only after they were married, and there was nothing in her attitude ahead of time to indicate what she would do? In that case, God was not to blame for his wife's departure, or more precisely, for not warning him that it would happen. If certain aspects of the future do not become definite until they actually occur, in particular human actions and decisions, then what the future held for him was not there for anyone to see, not even God.

Like the free will defense, then, open theodicy places responsibility for suffering on the unfortunate decisions of God's creatures rather than on God. Unlike many versions of free will theodicy, open theodicy maintains that free decisions remain indefinite until they occur. Consequently, they are not there to be known—they do not exist—until they are actually made. So not only is God not responsible for these decisions, God cannot be blamed for not knowing them, not preventing them or not warning us about them.

7

EVEN GOD CAN'T DO EVERYTHING

Finite God Theodicy

IN ONE OF THE "MY TURN" COLUMNS that appeared in *Newsweek* magazine for many years, Jayne Gilbert summed up her response to life's difficulties. "People often say that hard times build character," she wrote. "I think sometimes they're just hard times, and when they're over we move on in the best way we can. . . . Maybe this is what it means to finally become a grown-up—accepting that stuff happens. Some will be good and some will be bad, but for sure the route we're on is unpredictable."[1] In other words, ditch the explanations. Don't try to make sense of suffering, just try to get through it.

I suspect that lots of people share Gilbert's outlook. Not everyone finds a framework of meaning for their suffering or even looks for one. For many people, suffering just happens and that's it. The imperative they feel is not to understand it, but to survive it, and explanations are neither here nor there as far as they are concerned. They seem irrelevant to the real challenges of life.

This approach echoes one of the most popular books on suffering to appear within the past few decades. Harold Kushner's

---

[1]Jayne Gilbert, "The Family Car: A Metaphor for Life?" *Newsweek*, July 31, 2000, p. 14.

When Bad Things Happen to Good People was published over thirty years ago, but it is still widely read and discussed. When their son was three years old, the author and his wife learned that the boy had a rare disease called progeria, or rapid aging. Physicians told them that Aaron would never grow much beyond three feet in height, that he would look like a little old man while still a child, and that he would die in his early teens. The years passed and the dire predictions were all fulfilled. Aaron died two days after his fourteenth birthday.

Although Rabbi Kushner had always believed in God and devoted his life to helping others believe, the tragedy forced him, in his words, "to rethink everything he had been taught about God and God's ways." And in this book, dedicated to Aaron's memory, that is exactly what Kushner does. Like the other theodicies we have examined, this approach finds a way to put God and suffering in the same universe, but it does so in a notably nontraditional way.

The first thing Kushner does is reject all the explanations that make God the source of suffering—the theories that God is punishing us, teaching us or testing us by making us suffer. None of these are helpful, Kushner argues. In fact, they are not really intended to help us. Their real purpose is defend God, to get us to stop blaming God for our problems. When we properly understand suffering, according to these views, we will see that it is ultimately good for us, or at least good for the universe. In the wake of his enormous loss, Kushner found all such explanations completely unsatisfying, and he was forced to seek other ways to look at suffering.

One of the sources he examined was the biblical book of Job, the story of the good man who suffered terribly. And the conclusions he reached as he read this ancient classic differ from almost every other interpretation. Kushner observes that everyone in the book, Job and his friends included, wants to affirm three things: (1) God is all-powerful. God wills everything that happens; (2) God is just and fair, so people get what they deserve. God rewards the good and punishes the wicked; (3) Job is a good person. As long as Job's family is intact and he is healthy and wealthy, it is easy to believe all three. But when Job suffers, we have a problem. We can affirm only two of them. Job's friends accepted (1) and (2) and rejected (3). They believed that Job must have done something to bring his difficulties on himself. Job himself affirmed (1) and (3). He believed that God was all-powerful, and he insisted that he was a good man. So Job questioned God's justice. He concluded that God is so powerful that he doesn't have to be fair,[2] and he wished there was someone who could adjudicate his case against God (Job 31:35).

According to Kushner, the author of the book of Job has a different view of these matters. "Forced to choose between a good God who is not totally powerful, or a powerful God who is not totally good, the author of the book of Job chooses to believe in God's goodness."[3] On this view, Job is good and God is fair, but God is not all-powerful. There are things that even God can't do. This is the position that Kushner himself proposes. Contrary to conventional pictures of God, he maintains, there are limits to God's control over the world. God cannot do everything God would like to. God is on our side when bad things happen to us, of course. And God no doubt wishes there were more God could do to help us. But God is not to be blamed for our difficulties.

Of course, the fact that God can't do everything doesn't mean that God can't do anything. And the principal way God works in the world is through human beings. When we care for those around us who suffer we show that we are responsive to God's own values

---

[2]Harold S. Kushner, *When Bad Things Happen to Good People* (New York: Schocken Books, 1981), pp. 37-39, 42.
[3]Ibid., p. 43.

and purposes. In a manner of speaking, we serve as God's hands and feet. Because we occupy a different place in the scheme of things, we can do things that God can't.

Process Theodicy

There are a number of people whose response to suffering resembles Kushner's. Instead of looking for ways to reconcile suffering with God's power, they reconsider the nature of God's power. Among those who take this route is a group of contemporary thinkers known as "process philosophers." The most influential figures in the history of process thought were Alfred North Whitehead and Charles Hartshorne. The name itself reflects the title of Whitehead's seminal book *Process and Reality*.[4] The emphasis on process is also evident in the titles of some of Hartshorne's writings, such as *Reality as Social Process*.[5] A number of Christian thinkers find process philosophy helpful in their efforts to interpret the Christian faith, and their work is often described as "process theology." It is a well-known development in contemporary religious thought, particularly in Anglo-American circles during the middle to latter part of the twentieth century.[6]

---

[4]Alfred North Whitehead, *Process and Reality: An Essay in Cosmology* (1929; repr., New York: Free Press, 1969). This famous book is based on the Gifford Lectures that Whitehead delivered at the University of Edinburgh in 1927–1928.

[5]Charles Hartshorne, *Reality as Social Process: Studies in Metaphysics and Religion* (New York: Hafner, 1971). Hartshorne is also known for his vigorous defense of the ontological argument—see *Anselm's Discovery: A Re-examination of the Ontological Proof of God's Existence* (LaSalle, IL: Open Court, 1965) and *The Logic of Perfection and Other Essays in Neoclassical Metaphysics* (LaSalle, IL: Open Court, 1962). But he develops a number of other theistic proofs as well—see, for example, "Six Theistic Proofs" in *Creative Synthesis and Philosophic Method* (LaSalle, IL: Open Court, 1970), chap. 14.

[6]Among contemporary process theologians, John B. Cobb Jr., Schubert M. Ogden and David Griffin are particularly well known, although Ogden is critical of the expression "process theology." For methodological reasons, Ogden holds that theology should be identified as "theology," pure and simple, and should not be conflated with a particular philosophical position, no matter how helpful it may be.

From the perspective of process thought, God is deeply involved in the world. God cares about it, God is responsive to it, and God works hard to reach the divine objectives for it. But there is only so much that God can do. God doesn't have the sort of power that enables God to achieve everything God wants just by willing it to be so, or by directly, unilaterally, acting within the world to accomplish it. From a process perspective, the idea that God can do anything God wants to do, along with the related idea that God is therefore responsible for everything, is a colossal mistake.[7] It misconstrues God's actual role in the world.

Let's take a moment to fill in this sketch. As the name indicates, process thinkers view reality as a social process. Momentary events, rather than enduring objects, are the fundamental constituents of reality. And this reverses the way we typically think about things. From a conventional perspective, the world consists of objects that come into existence and endure for a time, and are more or less the same as long as they last. Events happen to objects, but objects are the basic elements in reality. For process thought, however, events are more fundamental than objects. Indeed, an object is a linear society of events, or a series of events that share some enduring or defining characteristics. Reality as such consists of temporal process, according to which the world or universe represents an ongoing sequence, indeed an everlasting sequence, of an incalculable number of events.

An essential characteristic of these events is freedom, or self-determination. Some events have very little freedom. Their range of options is extremely limited. Others have a wide range of freedom. The events that make up the tree in my backyard, for example, have relatively little latitude in their decisions, while the possibilities available to a human being are vast and diverse.

---

[7]Charles Hartshorne makes this clear in the title of one of his later works, *Omnipotence and Other Theological Mistakes* (Albany, NY: SUNY Press, 1984).

A world conceived along such lines requires a supremely power-ful being, and God actively participates in the events that make up the world. In fact, God is absolutely necessary. One of God's func-tions is to place limits on the conflict that inevitably results when a welter of self-creative agents is at work. Otherwise, things could degenerate into sheer chaos. The application of God's power takes the form of persuasion, however, rather than coercion. God guides or influences the choice that constitutes each event. God seeks to lure, or nudge, each decision in one direction or another. But God cannot unilaterally impose God's will on them. The creatures all have their own integrity, and they make their own decisions. Con-sequently, there are significant limits to God's power. There are things God cannot do, not because God deliberately chooses to hold back, but because God does not have the kind of power it would take to do them.

We could use the expression "naturalistic theism" to describe this perspective. On this view, there is a God, a supreme personal being, and God is integral to the overall scheme of things, but the same "laws" that apply to everything in the universe also apply to God.[8] God can no more choose to suspend those laws than we can. According to process thinkers, ultimate reality is not just God, period, but God-and-the-world. God incorporates the world within the divine life. God is sensitive to the world of creaturely events, God cares about it, and to an extent God can influence what happens in it. While God is *involved* in every aspect of the world, however—sustaining, caring for and influencing it—God is unable to *interrupt* or intervene in the course of creaturely events. God cannot unilaterally bring about any specific state of affairs.

---

[8]In the words of one of Whitehead's often quoted statements, "God is not to be treated as an exception to all metaphysical principles, invoked to save their collapse. He is their chief exemplification" (*Process and Reality,* p. 405).

People who speak of God as sending or allowing natural disasters such as hurricanes and tidal waves are therefore mistaken. God did not cause the massive tsunami that swept into Southeast Asia in late 2004, the earthquake that devastated Haiti in 2010 or the tornados that destroyed towns in Oklahoma in 2013. Nor could God have prevented them. What happens in the earth's crust and atmosphere is determined by geological and meteorological factors, not theological ones. Can God stop a speeding bullet from taking the life of an innocent victim? Again, no. The laws of physics determine what happens when someone fires a loaded gun. God abhors violence, and God may try to persuade a person to refrain from pulling the trigger. But if a gunman resists God's influence, the bullet makes its way from the barrel to its object, and there is nothing God can do to stop it. So God does not act *within* the world alongside the creatures. God's actions occupy a different level of reality.

An illustration from sports may be helpful here. Suppose we are watching a major league baseball game. On the most obvious level, the game involves a number of players who are throwing, hitting and catching a baseball. But there are others who are involved in the game as well. There is the manager of each team who decides which players take the field. There is the owner of the team, who may also own the stadium it plays in. He pays the players' salaries, provides their uniforms and equipment, and covers their travel expenses. There is the person who invented the game to begin with, and there are the authorities who modify the rules from time to time. There are umpires on the field, whose job is to ensure that the game is played according to the rules. We may even want to include the spectators, who watch the action with interest.

The players on the field are the only ones who actually throw, hit and catch the baseball. Managers can send in signals, make changes in the line-up and so on, but they can't go into the game and actually try to make the plays. And with few exceptions,[9] owners don't make decisions about who enters a game either. That's the manager's job. So, when a batter gets a hit, he gets the credit, not the manager or the owner or the umpire. And when a batter strikes out, it is his fault, not someone else's.

According to process thought, God's role in the world is a little like that of the owner or manager of a baseball team, or perhaps the inventor of the game. But it is unlike that of the players. God doesn't "enter the game," so to speak, on that level of participation. God cannot unilaterally cause things to happen in the realm of our ordinary physical experience. God has hopes for the creatures, God does everything God can to exert a positive influence on their decisions, and God is genuinely affected by what they do. But God is not responsible for any specific events that occur. Indeed, nothing that happens is attributable directly to divine activity. To quote Hartshorne, "The only livable doctrine of divine power is that it influences all that happens but determines nothing in its concrete particularity." Consequently, "it is the existence of many decision makers that produces everything, whether good or ill."[10]

This view of things has important implications for human suffering. From a process perspective, the problem of evil is really a pseudoproblem. It arises from a mistaken view of God's place in the scheme of things. God is a being of great power, but everything else has a degree of power too, and God is not in a position to determine what each agent does. In a world where all sorts of decisions take place, suffering is inevitable, because there is no way to avoid conflicts among them.

One of the most prevalent reasons people give for embracing the process perspective is the conviction that it relieves God of any respon-

---

[9]George Steinbrenner, late owner of the New York Yankees, comes to mind.
[10]Hartshorne, *Omnipotence*, pp. 25, 18.

sibility for suffering, in direct contrast to divine omnipotence as traditionally understood. A literally "all-powerful" being could produce any state of affairs it wanted to. It could create an entire world devoid of suffering, and it could prevent every specific instance of suffering. If indeed God has that kind of power, some process thinkers insist, then God must be morally culpable for failing to use it, and God is worthy of blame for everything that goes wrong.[11] In addition, they sometimes add, such a concept of God would remove from us all responsibility, and all incentive, to better the world we live in. If there is nothing God can't do, there is really no reason for us to do anything.

Although the seminal figures in process thought were philosophers rather than theologians, their descriptions of God connect rather directly with some important features in the biblical portrait. According to process philosophers and theologians alike, love is God's defining characteristic. And as we have seen, some of the most memorable passages in the New Testament contain emphatic affirmations of God's love, including these: "For God so loved the world that he gave his only Son, so that everyone who believes in him may not perish but may have eternal life" (Jn 3:16), and "Whoever does not love does not know God, for God is love" (1 Jn 4:8). For process thinkers, divine love takes the form of intense interest and intimate involvement in the creaturely world.

One theologian who seeks to integrate the biblical emphasis on divine love with the categories of process thought is Daniel Day Williams, author of *The Spirit and the Forms of Love*.[12] For Williams, love is indispensable to an understanding of both God and humanity,[13]

---

[11]David Ray Griffin, "Creation Out of Chaos and the Problem of Evil," in *Encountering Evil: Live Options in Theodicy,* ed. Stephen T. Davis (Louisville, KY: John Knox Press, 1981), p. 104. For a fuller account of Griffin's views, see *God, Power, and Evil: A Process Theodicy* (Philadelphia: Westminster Press, 1976).

[12]Daniel Day Williams, *The Spirit and the Forms of Love* (New York: Harper & Row, 1968).

[13]"If love constitutes God's being, and if man is created in the image of God, then the key

and love should therefore be central to our interpretation of Christian doctrines, especially such fundamental doctrines as the incarnation and the atonement. Accordingly, he describes the incarnation as "the communion of God with the man whose vocation is to enact love in the world."[14] And, in contrast to traditional theories of atonement, he finds the clue to God's dealing with human guilt and self-destruction in the "experience of reconciliation between persons."[15] In the suffering of Jesus Christ, Williams insists, we see the suffering of God— an idea that traditional theories avoided, with their insistence that the Father does not suffer. "If God does not suffer," he asserts, "then his love is separated completely from the profoundest human experiences of love, and the suffering of Jesus is unintelligible as the communication of God's love to man."[16]

This intimate connection between divine and human is typical of the process view of God. For process thought, God is to be understood entirely with reference to God's experience of the world. Not only is God intimately involved in the world, as Williams's reflections indicate, and not only does God's experience include the events of the world, but the reality, the very being, of God is inconceivable apart from the world. In other words, God's own existence requires the existence of a creaturely world.

ATTRACTIONS OF FINITE GOD THEODICY

What Kushner and process thinkers alike propose is the concept of a finite God—a God whose role in the overall scheme of things is enormously important, but not the role that more traditional views

---

to man's being and to God's being is the capacity for free, self-giving mutuality and concern for the other" (ibid., p. 160).

[14]Ibid., p. 185.

[15]Ibid., p. 176.

[16]Ibid., p. 185.

of God envision.[17] Such a God can do many things, indeed God exercises cosmic functions, but God cannot do the sorts of things that people traditionally expect God to do or certainly hope God will do. Many people find this view of God attractive, because it removes from God any responsibility for human suffering. But for others, it creates some serious problems.

The most obvious benefit of a finite God theodicy is the fact that it relieves God of responsibility for suffering. God simply does not have the sort of power that enables God to cause or prevent things from happening on the level of our ordinary human experience.

A finite God theodicy also provides a powerful incentive for us to do everything we ourselves can do to relieve suffering and make the world a safer and saner place to live. God's activity within the world always involves the creatures—indeed, it takes place only through creaturely participation—and this places great significance on human cooperation with God. Much as God may oppose the forces of disease and destruction, God cannot do our work for us. God cannot jump in and dramatically change our circumstances. It is our responsibility to care for our planet. Famine, pestilence, global warming—if there are solutions to these problems, it is up to us to find them. They will not miraculously drop from the sky. It is our job to make the world a better place. We must find cures for disease, we must address the ills of society, and we must find ways to relieve the tensions that lead to conflict and war. If God does not have the power to intervene, then the future of our planet is in our hands. We cannot look to God to bail us out.[18]

---

[17]Though it shares a number of features of these views. Hartshorne identifies his view of God as "neoclassical," for example.

[18]Cf. one of David Ray Griffin's objections to the classic view of divine omnipotence: "It encourages complacency about the future of our planet." "Process Theology and the Christian Good News," in *Searching for an Adequate God: A Dialogue Between Process and Free Will Theists,* ed. John B. Cobb Jr. and Clark H. Pinnock (Grand Rapids: Eerdmans, 2000), p. 24.

Finite God theodicy not only provides us with an incentive to seek the betterment of human life, it also calls us to lives of personal courage. Suffering is an inescapable part of existence. To some degree everything suffers. Pain and loss are a part of life and we simply have to deal with them. There is no point in wasting our energy vainly wishing for a different kind of world.

The concept of a finite God also relieves us of a persistent perplexity facing people of faith. It's what some call "the morality of selective intervention."[19] If we believe that God performs miracles, the obvious question is why we don't see more of them. And why does God intervene just when and where God does? Why, for example, doesn't God heal more sick and dying children? And if God can heal one person, why doesn't God heal everyone who is sick? Why didn't God stop the bullet that struck President Kennedy? And why didn't God divert the planes that flew into the Pentagon and the World Trade Center on 9/11? Better yet, why didn't God prevent the hijackers from boarding these planes in the first place?

Sometimes stories of answered prayer only intensify this problem. One I remember hearing as a child described a boy named Joe who was devastated when he lost a precious quarter someone had given him. He searched for it all day without success and finally, at bedtime, he knelt down and asked God to help him find it. At that very moment, he felt something hard and flat under his knee. He reached down and picked up his missing coin.

If God will help a distressed child find a twenty-five-cent piece, people are bound to wonder, why doesn't God use such power to meet vastly greater needs? Why didn't God do more to help the millions of people who have died of AIDS since the early eighties? There seems to be no good way to explain why God would intervene

---

[19] I'm indebted to my colleague David R. Larson for this expression.

in one case but not in the others. I know two men whose wives had breast cancer. Each prayed earnestly for his wife to be healed. One woman died; the other recovered. What explains the difference? It doesn't seem fair for God to answer some prayers and ignore others.

With a finite God, these difficulties dissolve. There is a simple explanation for God's apparent absence. God doesn't intervene, not because God doesn't want to or doesn't care to or for some arcane reason that leaves us questioning God's motives. God doesn't intervene because God doesn't have that sort of power. God does not have the ability to reach in and interrupt the natural course of events.

QUESTIONS ABOUT FINITE GOD THEODICY

In its attempt to solve some of the problems associated with suffering, the notion of a finite God raises some serious questions. While it gives us a powerful incentive to do what we can to make the world better, it leaves us wondering about the future. If, in fact, we are "on our own" in the world, and God is essentially a caring spectator, our fate is no different from that of everything in the world around us. Like all objects in the physical world, our bodies cannot last forever. Nor can the human race as a whole. According to conventional cosmology, our planet is headed for extinction. In time, the sun will grow larger, the earth will become uninhabitable, and eventually the solar system will disappear. Granted, that's several billion years away, but it is inevitable nonetheless. As for the universe as a whole, it too is headed for destruction. Whether it ends with a bang or a whimper depends on which version of the Big Bang theory you subscribe to. It will either collapse on itself (the big crunch) or continue expanding until it finally dissipates (the big freeze). Neither scenario provides for a continuation of human life as we know it. Whatever phase of cosmic evolution follows, it seems, it will not include us.

If, as process thought maintains, God is not in a position to alter the physical factors that ordinarily bring our lives to an end after seven or eight decades, it seems unlikely that God has the power to restore or extend our existence in some future state. But process thinkers are not agreed on the issue. For some of them, life here and now is enough. In fact, they argue that it is presumptuous for anyone to expect more. The Creator, not the creature, is meant to live forever. Moreover, they maintain that unending existence is not necessary in order for human life to have lasting meaning. Human beings have *objective* but not *subjective* immortality. That is to say, our lives have enduring significance because they make a permanent contribution to God's experience—because they endure forever in God's memory—but not because they go on and on.[20] In contrast, other process thinkers embrace the hope that our lives, in some form or other, will continue beyond death.[21]

Even if we grant that life here and now can be enough, we have to consider the vast discrepancies that characterize human life in this world. A small percentage of the human race now lives in relative comfort. For those who enjoy a relatively full life, that may be enough. But for millions of impoverished human beings, and for the untold numbers who suffer physically and

---

[20]Process thinkers such as Charles Hartshorne and Schubert Ogden find the concept of personal immortality problematic for other reasons as well. One is the possibility that unending existence is undesirable. Sooner or later we would inevitably run out of things to interest us and life would become a drag. Then too there are persistent challenges facing any attempt to conceive a future beyond death. If humans are material beings who exist in a material world, and we need bodies to live, how would someone's future body be related to one's body in this life? How would a replica of my physical body actually represent a continuation of *my* life? And if the reply comes that humans can exist in some immaterial form, then we face another challenge: the mounting evidence from neuroscience demonstrates that brain and mind—brain and person, indeed—are inextricably connected. So a bodiless human being is essentially inconceivable.

[21]John B. Cobb Jr., for example.

emotionally, it isn't. Many will hope for a God who can do more than a finite God theodicy provides.

There are a number of thinkers who agree with process thought that God does not for the most part intervene or interfere in the natural course of events, but they view this as a matter of divine policy rather than metaphysical necessity. God has the power to intervene, they maintain, but God exercises this power sparingly, out of respect for the freedom God grants the creatures. Rather than acting unilaterally in the world, God typically interacts with the creatures.

As with other approaches to suffering, the finite God perspective exhibits both attractive and problematic features. It avoids or "dissolves" some of the problems that a traditional concept of divine omnipotence generates, but it also removes some of its reassuring features. Some people, such as Kushner, are willing to pay this price. When faced with his son's devastating physical condition, he found that responses to the problem of evil that had previously satisfied him intellectually were not helpful on a personal level. Eventually, he came to an understanding of God that made the crisis he faced comprehensible, and it involved the idea that God does not have the kind of power envisioned by traditional definitions of omnipotence.

Other people find that a position like Kushner's is not helpful when they face suffering. They may not be able to explain why it is that God allows them to suffer, but they nevertheless draw assurance from the thought that God has the sort of power that will eventually overcome and eradicate suffering. Their experiences illustrate a profound paradox. The concepts of divine power and goodness that make suffering such a formidable challenge on an intellectual level are the very qualities that many find most reassuring on a personal level. They may not be able to explain why a

God who is infinite in power and goodness allows creatures to suffer, but when they encounter suffering they find comfort in the thought that there is a God who has these qualities.[22]

Looking Back

Our review of different theodicies as they are generally known has taken us down a number of different paths. As we have seen, some people place suffering squarely within God's will for us. They believe that divine power is so extensive that it includes everything that happens, good and bad alike. So even life's worst experiences serve God's exalted purpose. Others take the view that God does not plan every instance of suffering, but God created a world where suffering would exist because it is the ideal environment for soul making or character development. Whether or not suffering is good in itself, according to these views, it contributes to a greater good.

Still others maintain that suffering is not something God wants for us. It results from the mistakes that some of God's creatures have made. Even so, however, it does not ultimately thwart God's will. God reacts to suffering by trying to mitigate its consequences and bring about good things anyway. Things that aren't good in themselves can nevertheless contribute to something good because God creatively responds to them. In fact, God is so resourceful that nothing is too negative for God to use for a positive purpose. Nothing lies outside God's capacity to work for good.

At the same time, the extent of the good that God can achieve depends on the sort of power God has. For more traditional views of the divine, God has the sort of power that makes it possible for

---

[22]Cf. Langdon Gilkey, "Those very facets of the idea of creation which made evil absolutely inexplicable, the transcendent power of God, the goodness of creation, and the love of God, were the ultimate principles according to which the fear and dread of evil were conquered in Christian spirits." *Maker of Heaven and Earth: A Study of the Christian Doctrine of Creation* (Garden City, NY: Anchor Books, 1965), p. 223.

God to transform the order of things and eventually bring an end to pain and suffering. For process or limited God theodicy, power is more widely dispersed in the universe, and omnipotence as traditionally defined is not the kind of power that any single being could have, not even God.

These are just some of the ways that thoughtful people have tried to show that suffering can exist in God's world, that suffering is not incompatible with the reality of a supreme personal being. For other thinkers, however, all such attempts are unconvincing. As they see it, the only thing harder to accept than suffering itself is the idea that suffering is compatible with the existence of God.

In our quest for a practical theodicy, we face a complex challenge. On the one hand, we want to be intellectually responsible. We want our views of God and God's relation to the world to be clear and consistent. If things utterly fail to make sense to us, there is no way they could provide us a basis for living constructively. We can't believe in things we find unbelievable, even if we want to. On the other hand, we also need beliefs that give us reassurance, beliefs that help us respond to suffering resourcefully. Fulfilling both imperatives is not easy, and most people live with a compromise of sorts. They find that certain ideas are helpful to them on a practical level and are generally intelligible, even though they may not cohere perfectly on a theoretical level. But they also find that they can live with the tension between them. Developing a practical theodicy will be the central concern of our concluding chapter.

8

RAGE AGAINST THE DYING OF THE LIGHT

Protest Theodicies

Julia Sweeney is a popular comedienne, best known as one of the regulars on *Saturday Night Live* in the early '90s. Once a devout Catholic, Sweeney lost her faith and is now openly critical of religion. In fact, she actively advocates atheism. An online article by Matthew Baldwin traces Sweeney's path as she moved from faith to outspoken unbelief through a series of jarring experiences.[1]

In 1994 Sweeney quit *Saturday Night Live* and "moved from New York back to Los Angeles, with high hopes for the future and for her forthcoming movie." Instead, as she later put it, 1994 turned out to be "the year that I became Job." First, the movie failed. "Then her younger brother was diagnosed with lymphatic cancer, and both he and her parents moved into Sweeney's LA home."

For therapeutic relief, Sweeney turned to stand-up comedy, where "she told personal stories of suffering, transforming pathos into deep comedy." Then in 1995 Sweeney herself was diagnosed with cancer. She began chemotherapy and underwent a series of

---

[1]Matthew Baldwin, "Julia Sweeney Says 'Ha!'" *Sightings*, May 25, 2006. All subsequent quotations related to Sweeney are from this article.

surgeries. Soon after, her brother died at the age of thirty-one. When her cancer went into remission, Sweeney "turned her stand-up material into a full length monologue, *God Said 'Ha!'*, which she took to theaters in New York, San Francisco and LA."

Through all these difficulties, Sweeney remained faithful to her religious upbringing. She reported finding solace in prayer, and despite feeling anger about certain aspects of Catholic dogma, she still attended mass. But then her faith left her. She explained this transformation in another monologue, *Letting Go of God*, which played for several years in theaters from Broadway to Hollywood.

In *God Said 'Ha!'* Sweeney toyed with the idea that God was playing a practical joke on her, but in *Letting Go of God* she leveled a searing and witty critique against religion. According to the monologue, she joins a church-led Bible study group, but the more she reads the Bible, the more questions it raises. She finds disturbing the accounts of Sodom and Gomorrah going up in flames, Abraham (almost) sacrificing Isaac, Jephthah sacrificing his daughter and Jesus cursing a fig tree.

She also finds that the Bible provides "no satisfactory response to her personal tragedies." She compares her brother's months of "unspeakable suffering" to Jesus' death and resurrection, which was relatively quick by comparison. Over time, she finds herself repulsed by the deity represented in the Bible's "nutty stories." "Finally, she accedes to a little voice inside that has been whispering, to her horror, "There is no God."

As her monolgue indicates, Sweeney turned her disillusionment with God into a force for atheism. According to Baldwin, she had "the evangelical zeal of a convert." She shared her experience on National Public Radio. She fought the religious right in radio ads. She spoke at a meeting of the International Atheist Alliance. The title of a book she wrote says it all—*My Beautiful Loss of Faith Story: A Memoir.*[2]

People who take the approaches to suffering we looked at in earlier chapters all share the conviction that it is possible somehow to reconcile a belief in God with the harsh realities of life. Whether they see suffering as inherently good or bad, they believe that believing in God can help us to face it.

Sweeney and others like her disagree with all these views. For them, suffering doesn't just make it difficult to believe in God; it makes believing in God impossible or nearly impossible. And all the measures philosophers have come up with to demonstrate that suffering is somehow compatible with God's existence only show how futile the attempt really is. Instead of proving that God and suffering can coexist, they actually prove the opposite. Moreover, they argue, attempts to demonstrate God's existence in spite of the pervasiveness of suffering are not merely unhelpful, they are an affront to those who suffer.

People who respond to evil and to theodicies with protest are seldom dispassionate. They are angry. They are upset not only with suffering, they are upset with those who are not upset with it—in particular with those who are smugly convinced that suffering somehow has a place in God's world. They find outrageous the idea that God wants or even allows us to suffer for some inscrutable reason. So conventional theodicies are not just logically or philosophically unconvincing, they are personally and morally offensive. In the face of sufferings so heinous we can hardly imagine them; attempts to rationalize them make no sense. We should reject them and encourage others to do the same.

Suffering doesn't turn everyone into an energetic atheist, but it raises serious doubts about God in the minds of a great many

---

[2]Julia Sweeney, *My Beautiful Loss of Faith Story: A Memoir* (New York: Henry Holt & Co., 2007).

people, and it often leaves them deeply dissatisfied with "logical" explanations. A college friend of mine who went on to study medicine, and got a law degree later on as well, graphically describes the way suffering has affected her view of God:

> My studies in science, my experiences in life and in medicine have not always reinforced religious faith. For many years, I had difficulty believing that God even exists, much less pays attention to the human condition. Although I now believe that it is "more likely than not" that there is a God, my doubts regarding his involvement in the world are still legion, often oppressive.
>
> The most serious barrier to belief, for me, remains the problem of pain, especially as I have seen it in the suffering of children. For a long time after my first leukemia patient died— she was a beautiful, frightened, four-year-old redhead named Amy—I had difficulty believing in God. One night in the hospital, she held my hand tightly and asked, "Am I going to die?" Perhaps sensing the affirmative in my hesitation, she added, "But Doctor C, I don't *want* to die. I'm afraid of the dark."
>
> I have also seen children who have been beaten and even tortured to death. My first child-abuse patient at Riverside General Hospital was a nine-month-old boy. Where, I wondered, was God when his parents were beating him?
>
> If there is a God, I had (and have) difficulty understanding His (or Her) priorities. God seems to have a major attention-deficit disorder. The answers of my theologian friends—that human freedom is the highest good, that divine self-restraint is of paramount importance in the celestial controversy between good and evil, that it is our response to suffering, not the pain itself, that matters—ring hollow within the echoing

walls of a morgue at the autopsy of a child. I understand why a friend of mine, another pediatric oncologist, once said to me, "Either there is no God, or if there is, I hate him for letting my patients suffer as they do."[3]

Nothing generates more dissatisfaction with traditional explanations for suffering than the misery of innocent, defenseless children. It gives rise to some of literature's most memorable challenges to religious belief.[4] In his novel, *The Plague,* Albert Camus describes the misery that afflicted the Algerian port of Oran during an outbreak of the bubonic plague. The city is under quarantine. No one can leave or enter, and the inhabitants are left to cope with their losses as best they can. The central character is a physician, Doctor Rieux, who fights a losing battle with the horrifying effects of the plague. Another important figure is Father Paneloux, a Catholic priest. Both do their best to respond to the disaster, but their approaches are strikingly different. The doctor tries to heal the sick, the priest tries to prepare the dying for eternity. The two confront each other in one of the narrative's most dramatic moments.

A child has just died and Doctor Rieux responds with a feeling of "mad revolt." Father Paneloux agrees that such a thing is "unbearable." Then he adds, "That sort of thing is revolting because it passes our human understanding. But perhaps we should love what we cannot understand." Rieux shook his head. "No, Father. I've a very different idea of love. And until my dying day I shall refuse to

---

[3]Donna Carlson, "My Journey of Faith in Medicine," unpublished manuscript, 1999.

[4]References to theodicy are not infrequent in serious fiction. For example, here is an exchange between two characters in New York City from a novel that appeared a few years after 9/11. Annabel: "Yesterday morning, I actually sort of prayed. I complained, anyway, to the God that doesn't exist. . . . Think of poor DeVaughn. He's been praying so far for nothing." Murray: "Which is why one shouldn't believe in God. . . . Because there is no answer to the problem of theodicy." Claire Messud, *The Emperor's Children* (New York: Vintage Books, 2007), p. 457.

love a scheme of things in which children are put to torture."[5]

A somewhat similar confrontation occurs in Dostoyevsky's novel, *The Brothers Karamazov*. Alyosha, a gentle soul who has entered a monastery, is deep in conversation with his brother Ivan, who seriously questions God's existence. To substantiate his doubts, Ivan describes a five-year-old girl whose "educated and well-bred" parents have brutally mistreated her. Angry because she didn't ask to get up and go to the bathroom in the middle of the night, "they beat her, flogged her, kicked her . . . until her whole body was nothing but bruises." Then they locked her in the freezing outhouse all night. After that, her mother smeared her faced with excrement and made her eat it.

Then Ivan turns to Alyosha with a question that has challenged believers for decades:

> "Imagine that you yourself are building the edifice of human destiny with the object of making people happy in the finale, of giving them peace and rest at last, but for that you must inevitably and unavoidably torture just one tiny creature, that same child who was beating her chest with her little fist, and raise your edifice on the foundation of her unrequited tears— would you agree to be the architect on such conditions? Tell me the truth."
>
> "No, I would not agree," Alyosha said softly.[6]

As Ivan's challenge suggests, few things are as wrenching to us, or as intellectually disturbing, as the suffering of a child, especially when it is deliberately inflicted and even more so when the tormentors are family. In fact a child's suffering is the palmary instance

---

[5] Albert Camus, *The Plague*, trans. Stuart Gilbert (New York: Vintage Books, 1972), pp. 202-3.
[6] Fyodor Dostoyevsky, *The Brothers Karamazov: A Novel in Four Parts with Epilogue*, trans. Richard Pevear and Larissa Volokhonsky (New York: North Point, 1990), p. 245.

of unjust and unjustifiable suffering. When people object to the idea of God, the spectacle of suffering children is one of the most frequent reasons they give. What could possibly justify the torture of a little girl? For Ivan, not even the security of the entire universe! If a single instance of parental cruelty is enough to raise questions about God's existence, suffering on a massive scale completely undermines it. Either way, it is hard to place the misery of children, whatever its extent, within any version of a "greater good theodicy."

Though Dostoyevsky's Ivan and Camus's Rieux both interact with religious figures in the passages described, there are notable variations in two scenes. In one, a child suffers at the hands of her monstrous parents. In the other, many children suffer from a painful and fatal infection. The first is an example of moral evil; the second, of natural evil—to invoke a distinction philosophers often make. The sort of anger or outrage the two express is different too. Ivan is incensed with a particular concept or picture of God that supposedly makes the little girl's plight comprehensible. Rieux steadfastly refuses to accept an indifferent, unsympathetic universe. The doctor is not interested in such schemes, either their supposed strengths or manifest weaknesses. He only knows that a child's suffering is unacceptable and he is determined to alleviate it.

The Appeal of Protest Theodicy

It is hard not to feel the force of Camus's and Dostoyevsky's challenges. The most natural response to a child's suffering, particularly when it is willfully inflicted, is outrage pure and simple. And our minds balk at the thought that something could ever make it right. Such instances of suffering seem to defy all attempts to place them within some cosmic framework of meaning.

And even though we know that terrible things happen to children, every once in a while something comes along that seems to reach a new low. Several years ago the Associated Press reported the case of a father in Indiana who confessed to killing his infant son. The child's death was originally attributed to sudden infant death syndrome, but the man later told the police he planned the whole thing months in advance.

When his father died, he said, his fiancée refused to return from a vacation to be with him, and he determined to get even with her. He waited until they were married and had a child. After the baby was born he gave his wife time to get deeply attached to him. Then one afternoon he suffocated the infant in his crib. He said he wanted his wife to know what he felt like when his father died. Several months later remorse caught up with the man, and he admitted what he had done.[7]

How does this story affect you? Are you horrified? Outraged? Of course. We can't imagine any other reaction. And it is even harder to fit something like this into a theological or philosophical theory. How could God's plans for the world include the senseless death of an undeserving and uncomprehending child? And how could anything imaginable possibly bring good out of such cruelty? It is not hard to see why people are turned off by attempts to account for such suffering. Their brutal honesty is attractive. But it also raises some interesting questions.

What's Puzzling About Protest Theodicy

No response to suffering seems as straightforward and clear as protest theodicy. It expresses our spontaneous reaction to violence, pain and death. Nothing is more natural than to condemn suffering and refuse any attempt to explain or rationalize it, especially when it involves the suffering of the innocent and defenseless. Yet, as

---

[7]Associated Press, "Indianian Admits Fathering, Then Killing Child to Get Back at Wife," *Los Angeles Times*, June 28, 1999.

understandable as feelings of outrage at horrible happenings are, there's a rather striking paradox involved in using them to reject God. For instead of giving us reasons to object to the existence of God, such feelings, when carefully examined, actually support it.

When we condemn human cruelty, we are implicitly comparing what people actually do with what we believe they should do. In other words, we are invoking a standard of behavior that we expect human beings to meet and using it to evaluate their actions. Rather than take his baby's life, we believe, the Indiana father should have loved and cared for his child. His actions violated an obligation he should have met.

This raises an important question, however. What is the basis of this comparison? Who says it is better to love and nurture an infant than snuff out its life? Where does this criterion of human behavior come from? We can think of several possible answers. One, it is just a human convention. It is statistically the case that most parents care for their children. They house them, feed them, clothe them, cuddle them and play with them. And when they get sick, they worry about them and take them to the doctor. But that's not true of everyone. Some people neglect their children, a few abuse them and a small minority kill them. Are these parental behaviors mere deviations from the norm, or is something more involved?

It is also possible to describe our outrage in the face of cruelty as nothing more than an emotional reaction, as the mere expression of a personal preference. As if we were saying, in rather strong terms of course, "I'm personally repelled by such behavior. It's not the sort of thing that appeals to me." We all have personal likes and dislikes. I have never been able to drink buttermilk, to cite a trivial example. Everyone I know enjoys it, but I can't stand the taste. I don't like infanticide either. In fact, I find the thought of killing a child repulsive. But even though I dislike both buttermilk and infanticide, I would never put these reactions on the same level. One is a personal preference, the other is a deep-seated conviction. With enough effort, I can imagine developing a taste for buttermilk, but I can't imagine changing my attitude toward killing babies.

When we condemn people who abuse a child, then, we are not just making the observation that their parenting is "unorthodox," that their way of dealing with children is out of the mainstream or fails to conform to typical patterns of behavior. Nor are we simply saying, "We personally don't care for that sort of thing. We feel better when we see people looking after their kids." No, when we react with revulsion to child abuse, we are not just observing or dispassionately commenting on the behavior of the perpetrators, we are *condemning* their actions. We are judging their behavior to be morally reprehensible. We are insisting that it is wrong, not just for us or for our society, but for anyone anywhere under any circumstances to treat children that way. And when we do this, we are evaluating their actions in light of something independent of personal preference or the norms of conventional behavior. We are appealing to an objective moral standard. The intensity of our condemnation has no other explanation.

The next thing to ask is what this standard represents or where the standard comes from. We certainly experience it as something other than a private preference, a social convention or a statistical norm. As we experience it, the moral obligation to care for children is as much a part of "the way things are" as, say, the law of gravity. In other words, it has "objective" validity. It's not a human invention or a human convention. It's not just a way of looking at things, it's a statement about something that is always true: *it is wrong to torture children.* And the fact that some people miserably fail to live up to it doesn't alter the fact that they should.

But how could a moral obligation be "objective"—as objective, say, as the law of gravity or the mathematical truth that two and two make four? Only if morality somehow belongs to the very fabric of reality, or to turn it around, only if the fabric of reality is moral in nature. But that would be the case only if ultimate reality is personal in nature. Or, to put it another way, only if there is a God, a supreme personal being. After all, we don't feel responsible to things, we feel responsible to persons. And as described by most religious traditions, particularly those in the West, moral goodness is an essential characteristic of God. God is conceived as both the source and object of moral responsibility. God established the moral law, God placed within us an awareness of this law, and God will judge our actions by this law.

What protest theodicy presents us with, then, is a remarkable inconsistency. Our instinctive condemnation of human cruelty necessarily implies the existence of a supreme moral being. Yet this is the very idea that protest theodicy rejects! If something like torturing a child is wrong—not just unfortunate or unpleasant or atypical—but wrong, period, then it violates an essential standard of human behavior, an objective obligation. And the only way to account for such a standard is to attribute it to a transcendent source of moral obligation, to a supreme lawgiver, in other words, to God. Any alternative trivializes our moral convictions.

This is how Alvin Plantinga makes the point. Of all the arguments against God, he states, "only the argument from evil deserves to be taken really seriously. But I also believe, paradoxically enough, that there is a *theistic* argument *from* evil." The worst thing we can imagine is human wickedness, says Plantinga, "taking pleasure in the sufferings of others." It strikes us "as deeply perverse, wholly wrong, warranting not just quarantine and the attempt to overcome it, but blame and punishment." But a purely naturalistic perspective, a view of the world that excludes God, has "no place for genuine moral obligation of any sort." Therefore, "it has no place for such a category as horrifying wickedness. . . . There can be such a thing only if there is a way rational creatures are *supposed* to live, *obliged* to live." But that kind of normativity requires a law-giver, "one whose very nature it is to abhor wickedness."[8]

Those who embrace a theodicy of protest, therefore, face a di-lemma. Their outrage at suffering, particularly the suffering of children, leads them to reject the idea of God. But such outrage makes sense only if there is a God. Moral outrage implies that a moral order has been violated. But if there is a moral order, there must be a moral orderer, a person of supreme power and goodness who made the rules that people break and who holds them ac-countable for their actions. Take away the orderer and the order goes with it. And then there is no justification for the outrage. People may find cruelty unappealing, it may not be a course of action they choose to pursue, but they have no basis for morally condemning those who do.

On careful inspection, then, we see that theodicies of protest actually support the very idea they explicitly reject. They object to the idea of God in the name of moral outrage, but such outrage makes sense only if there is a God. One of Dostoyevsky's biogra-phers makes this point in a comment on Ivan's famous exchange with Alyosha in *The Brothers Karamazov*. "What provides Ivan's monologue its still undiminished power is the relentless rejection of God's world in the name of the very morality of love and com-passion that Christ himself brought into it."[9]

Still, it is worth noting in connection with protest theodicy that a refusal to accept suffering, especially the suffering of innocents,

---

[8]Alvin Plantinga, "A Christian Life Partly Lived," in *Philosophers Who Believe: The Spiritual Journeys of Eleven Leading Thinkers*, ed. Kelly James Clark (Downers Grove, IL: Inter-Varsity Press, 1993), pp. 72-73.

[9]Joseph Frank, *Dostoyevsky: A Writer in His Time* (Princeton, NJ: Princeton University Press, 2010), p. 872.

is something that religious and nonreligious people can fully share. Whatever the differences in their worldviews, people can unite in opposition to suffering and in seeking to change the factors that bring it about. In December 2012 the unthinkable happened at a Connecticut elementary school. A deranged young man, armed to the teeth, took the lives of twenty-six people, twenty of them very young children. Not long afterward, the grieving parents and others joined in calling for better background checks for gun purchases and bans on the sort of weapons that make such carnage possible. Religious and philosophical differences were inconsequential. They were united in their horror at such loss of life and in their determination to do something to prevent it from happening again.

9

FRAGMENTS OF MEANING

When Suffering Comes to You

INTO THE WILD, A BOOK BY JON KRAKAUER, tells the tragic story of Christopher McCandless, a young man from a well-to-do family who hitchhiked to Alaska in 1992 and vanished in the wilderness north of Denali. Four months later, his decomposed body was found by a party of moose hunters, along with some pictures he had taken. When the terrible news reached his mother, it was all she could do to examine the fuzzy snapshots of her son's last days. From time to time she broke down, and her weeping, in the author's words, expressed "a sense of loss so huge and irreparable that the mind balks at taking its measure. Such bereavement, witnessed at close range, makes even the most eloquent apologia for high-risk activities ring fatuous and hollow."[1]

In the vortex of great suffering any theodicy can seem fatuous and hollow. Even when time puts a loss like this into some sort of perspective, no explanation accounts for it. "I just don't understand why he had to take those kinds of chances," Billie McCandless protested through her tears. "I just don't understand it at all."

---

[1]Jon Krakauer, *Into the Wild* (Garden City, NY: Anchor Books, 1996), p. 132.

No matter how carefully we hone our thinking, no theory will ever make perfect sense of suffering, especially when we are the ones who suffer or the sufferer is someone we love. This is why finding a theodicy you can actually live by is never easy.

We have covered a lot of ground in our "theodicy review"—our look at different responses to suffering. But our work is not finished. It's not enough to canvas an array of theological and philosophical positions and leave things there. When it comes to suffering, the "so what?" questions are the most important ones of all. Now that we have seen what others have said about suffering, it's time for us to think about our own response, to begin looking for things that could help us face the serious challenges that suffering sooner or later brings to everyone.

Different Reasons for Different Views

There are several reasons that we looked at various views of suffering. One, of course, is the simple fact that different interpretations exist, and they all have important things to say. Every serious response to the questions that suffering raises—*What kind of world did God create? And what kind of God created the world?*—deserves to be taken seriously. As we have seen, each of them has both intellectual and personal dimensions. A great deal of reflection lies behind each of them, and they all have significant practical implications. What we think about suffering in general and how we experience suffering ourselves are intimately related.

Something else that led us to examine a variety of theodicies is the fact that suffering people draw personal strength from radically diverse approaches. While some of the theodicies we have described have certain features in common—a number of them embrace a rather strong notion of creaturely freedom, for example—the contrasts between others are striking. And as we have seen, the very idea that gives one sufferer comfort may not be helpful to another. Indeed, as Jim and Sharon Harris discovered, unwelcome explanations for suffering may only increase someone's pain. When it comes to a personal theodicy, there is no such thing as "one size fits all."

There is a third reason to consider different interpretations of suffering: they all have their limits. No theodicy perfectly maps the landscape of suffering, no matter how expansive or refined it may be. Every explanation leaves something unaccounted for. As Billie McCandless reminds us, great losses never make complete sense, no matter how hard we try to understand them. And this is true on both an intellectual and a personal level. We saw that every explanation of suffering, every theodicy we examined, leaves certain questions unanswered. And, as Harold Kushner found, the explanations for suffering that seemed satisfactory to him as a rabbinical student and then as a rabbi failed him when he learned that his son had a rare and fatal physical condition.

This brings us to a fourth reason to look at different views of suffering. Just as every interpretation is less than complete, every personal reaction will be less than perfectly coherent. As we have seen, suffering poses a profound threat to life's meaning. It typically leaves us bewildered and afraid. So, when suffering comes, we instinctively reach out for something, sometimes anything, that promises a measure of comprehension and reassurance. And we are less than concerned that the ideas or convictions we cling to fit perfectly together in a tidy logical package. This is almost certainly the case in the immediate aftermath of a great loss, but it may prove true over the long haul as well. On the one hand, we want things clear and simple for our minds to grasp. On the other, we need these ideas to have some "cash value" or "takeaway" on a personal basis. So what we are looking for at this stage in our discussion is an approach to suffering that is both intellectually attractive and personally encouraging, a theodicy that not only helps us wrap our minds around it—that makes some sort of sense to us—but also provides us with comfort and hope. What we need, in a word, is a "practical theodicy."

But what does a practical theodicy consist of? How do we go about drawing from the various interpretations of suffering available to us features that will actually help us when we are the ones who suffer? I believe that the various theodicies we have been looking at can provide a helpful resource. As we have seen, they have all attracted significant scholarly attention. But we have also noticed that each of these theodicies has practical appeal as well. At some time, someone somewhere has found something in every one of them that helps when facing a personal crisis. The question is how to bring the best of our ideas to bear on the most pressing of our personal needs.

In a collection of essays titled *Pain Seeking Understanding*, Larry D. Bouchard uses the expression "holding fragments" to describe a helpful approach to our problem.[2] Such an approach will acknowledge both the shattering, fragmenting effects of suffering on our lives and the fragmentary nature of our responses to it. The key to developing a practical theodicy is to assemble these pieces in ways that prove personally beneficial. Bouchard suggests that we start by identifying the "particular expressions of harm and contradiction" that arise from our suffering, then set the insights they provide beside "the fragmentary character of religious discernment." In other words, we should carefully note both the personal impressions that our suffering generates and the religious or philosophical convictions we have, and then

---

[2]Larry D. Bouchard, "Holding Fragments," in *Pain Seeking Understanding: Suffering, Medicine, and Faith*, ed. Margaret E. Mohrmann and Mark J. Hanson (Cleveland, OH: Pilgrim, 1999), pp. 13-28.

bring them together. Holding fragments, as Bouchard describes it, consists of "juxtaposing but not synthesizing fragmentary lives, traditions, and paths of thought."[3]

According to this description, the ingredients that go into a practical theodicy inevitably come from various and varying sources. In previous chapters, we looked at a number of different responses to the problem of suffering, noting some of the relevant philosophical arguments pro and con for each of them along with the reasons people find each helpful or not. We did this because the elements or fragments that form a practical theodicy come from both careful reflection and personal conviction, and because our most deeply held beliefs are typically based as much on intuition as rational investigation. Faced with suffering, people instinctively turn to long held religious beliefs, often beliefs they acquired during childhood. To be sure, the idea of God generates the most perplexing questions people ask when they consider the general phenomenon of suffering, but a belief in God brings strength to many when they themselves are the ones who suffer.

Philosopher Jeffrey Stout uses the French word *bricolage* to describe the sort of project we have in mind.[4] A *bricoleur* is a handyman who makes do with whatever materials he can find and patches things up with this and that. That's more or less what a practical theodicy does. It brings together fragments from different, sometimes widely scattered sources and applies them to pressing personal needs.

---

[3]Ibid., p. 13.

[4]Stout applies this expression to ethical discourse: "All great works of creative ethical thought (and some not so great) . . . involve moral *bricolage*. They start off by taking stock of problems that need solving and available conceptual resources for solving them. Then they proceed by taking apart, putting together, reordering, weighting, weeding out, and filling in." *Ethics After Babel: The Languages of Ethics and Their Discontents* (Boston: Beacon Press, 1988), p. 75.

As Bouchard reminds us, we cannot expect the fragments that come from such different sources to form a seamless whole. They won't fit together within a perfect, tightly knit, pattern. A practical theodicy is less like a puzzle with interlocking pieces than a quilt or a mosaic, whose component parts may differ markedly in size, shape, color and even material, yet nevertheless form an acceptable, sometimes even attractive, arrangement. Similarly, the disparate elements, the fragments, that people pull together from here and there as they search for ways to respond to suffering may lack perfect logical coherence and yet provide personal strength and reassurance. Their value lies in their overall effect, in the help they bring to real people facing real problems. If the outcome looks disorganized to some observers, that's to be expected. A practical theodicy will almost always contain diversity and tension. And this is where practical and theoretical theodicies differ.

As we noticed in our review of different theodicies, thinkers often develop one interpretation of suffering in direct opposition to others. They carefully delineate the factors that distinguish one view of suffering from another, emphasizing their differences. And they typically elevate one above the alternatives because it avoids certain logical pitfalls or evinces certain abstract values. To concrete sufferers, however, the differences among theodicies are less important than the various strengths they provide. Practical theology is by nature eclectic. It pulls together strands from various theodicies, even those that seem incompatible on a logical level. Variations, disparities, even contradictions, often appear among the elements of a practical theodicy.

A Personal Practical Theodicy

To develop a practical theodicy, a response to suffering that is personally helpful, we must draw together the fragments of meaning and reassurance that come to us from different directions and rather diverse sources. One source may be theodicies or theories of suffering like the ones we have been looking at. As we noted in chapter one, great suffering undermines our sense that life is meaningful, so a theory of ultimate meaning or a description of cosmic purpose can be helpful on a personal level.[5] It may help to make our suffering somewhat comprehensible. As we also noticed early on, the attempt to place our suffering within some large-scale framework of meaning or purpose is a natural part of the experience for many people, though not for everyone. As we have seen, there are some who resist the very idea that we can somehow make sense of suffering and others whose only objective is just to get through it. Still, suffering pushes most people to look for meaning, even people who are ordinarily disinclined to engage in serious reflection. We instinctively reach out for some cosmic perspective or worldview when suffering comes to us.

Another resource for practical theodicy consists in the stories of people who have suffered and survived, who have found meaning in the face of great suffering. So valuable are such accounts, in the view of some, that they not only represent a source of personal strength, they also help us to grapple with the philosophical issues that suffering raises. In her magisterial treatise *Wandering in Darkness*, Eleonore Stump asserts, "The difficult questions raised by the problem of suffering can be considered best in the context of narratives, especially biblical narratives." Indeed, "narrative makes a contribution to philosophical reflection that cannot be gotten as well, or at all, without the narrative."[6]

But the most prevalent, and for many the most influential, con-

---

[5] As my colleague David R. Larson has said, "Nothing is more practical than a good theory."

[6] Eleonore Stump, *Wandering in Darkness: Narrative and the Problem of Suffering* (New York: Oxford University Press, 2010), p. xviii.

tribution to a practical theodicy will be religion. Faced with suffering, people instinctively turn for reassurance to religious faith or to the religious tradition most familiar to them. And they characteristically look for ways to connect its most memorable strands—whether doctrines, symbols, stories, rituals or a mixture of them all—to the suffering they experience.

How then should we go about constructing a practical theodicy—a way to respond resourcefully to losses that threaten the very meaning of our lives?

Since a practical theodicy is highly personal, one way to round out our discussion would be for me to describe my own perspective on suffering as an example. I offer it as an illustration rather than a recommendation. Each of us has to make his or her own way through the challenges that suffering brings. But it is not a journey that anyone has to make alone, and we can all learn by tracing the paths that others have taken.

My own practical theodicy involves a number of deeply held convictions. Do these convictions of mine represent *logical* conclusions in the sense that they can be deductively or inductively derived from initial premises and joined together to form a coherent, cohesive, comprehensive theory? I doubt it. I believe there is solid evidence to support some of the elements in my theodicy, perhaps less for others. But that's the nature of a practical theodicy. It draws from various sources in the quest for something that works.

I studied theology for ten years in college, seminary and graduate school. Since then I've taught religion courses to college and university students for forty years or so. Raised in a conservative religious environment, I have been a convinced Christian for as long as I can remember and a lifelong church member. On the whole, my life has been pleasant, but not entirely trouble free. So the fragments that go into my own theodicy come from three identifiable sources—personal experience, religious nurture and intellectual reflection.

Let's start from the theoretical side. We have seen that people relate God to suffering in many different ways. One is to place suffering within God's will for us. For some who take this view, God's plan includes everything that happens, good and bad alike. For others God created a world where character development could take place, and this required a degree of suffering, though not necessarily all the suffering that actually occurs.

For several theodicies suffering lies outside God's will. Some of the creatures used the freedom God gave them to rebel instead of offering God their love and loyalty in return, and suffering is the consequence of their sad choices. God responds by seeking to mitigate the effects of suffering and achieve God's purposes for creation anyway. Among those who see suffering as opposed to God's will, there are those who maintain that God foresaw the occurrence of suffering in advance, decided to create a world with creaturely freedom anyway, and prepared to deal with it in positive ways when it occurred. For others in this general group, God knew that creaturely freedom involved the inherent risk of rebellion and resultant suffering, but did not know in advance whether or not the creatures would actually choose to rebel. And for some, human suffering results from a cosmic conflict that stems from superhuman rebellion against divine authority.

Then there are thinkers who draw rather different conclusions from the undeniable and pervasive reality of suffering. Since a God who is both perfectly good and supremely powerful could prevent or eliminate suffering and would surely want to do so, they conclude that God does not have that sort of ability. For some, this requires us to reinterpret the nature and scope of divine power. For others, it means that there is no God; in view of the massive suffering we see in the world the idea of God simply doesn't hold up.

For all but those in the very last of these groups, it is possible in one way or another to reconcile a belief in God with the harsh realities of life. Whether they place suffering inside or outside God's will, they believe that believing in God can help us to face it.

I find something of value in all of these diverse viewpoints. Each of them draws from the depths of human experience, and each expresses a heartfelt response to the challenges that suffering brings. I appreciate the confidence in the fulfillment of God's purposes that perfect plan theodicy exhibits; the affirmation of soul making theodicy that God uses suffering for positive purposes; the insistence that suffering is not what God intended for creation that is basic to the free will defense; the dramatic portrait of good versus evil that cosmic conflict theodicy paints; the conviction of open theists that God took a risk in creating beings who were significantly free; the realization that God does not always get God's way that finite God theodicy expresses; and the cry of outrage at innocent suffering that protest theodicy raises. So these are among the elements or fragments that I draw from these various perspectives on suffering.

Still, I am drawn to some of these views more than to others. I am one of those who believe that suffering is better understood as lying outside, rather than inside, God's will. I don't see how the vast scope and excruciating forms that suffering takes could be part of a perfect plan for creation. Instead, I believe that the risk of suffering came with the kind of world God decided to create, one with inhabitants who were significantly free. I also embrace the hope that suffering, horrible as it is, will not defeat God's purposes. God has the resources to counteract its effects and ultimately achieve God's goals for creation. So I find some philosophical treatments of the problem of suffering more convincing than others, even though they all have attractive features and they all raise challenging questions.

In developing a practical theodicy of your own, you may find it helpful to think about thoughtful approaches to suffering like these and others as well. Hard thinking about challenging issues is never easy, but there are times when it is important, and in the case of something as unavoidable and disruptive as suffering, it may be downright indispensable.

As we have seen, suffering raises large-scale questions about the nature of reality and the meaning of human existence—and these are the essential topics that religion deals with. Consequently, religious convictions play a natural role developing a practical theodicy.

When I turn to the religious resources that have always been a part of my life, I find that the central elements of the Christian story, in particular, the cross and the resurrection of Jesus, are also central to my practical theodicy. In a way reminiscent of Stump's suggestive account, this is the narrative, or the specific part of the Gospel narratives, that connects most directly with my own perspective on suffering. According to the canonical Gospels, Jesus approached the cross with fear and apprehension. During the last night of his life, he asked his closest friends to watch with him, and he fervently prayed that God would spare him the bitter cup set before him. Nevertheless, he accepted the fact that God's purposes were larger than his own preferences, so notwithstanding his hopes, he endured the agony of the cross. And his cry of desolation, "My God, my God, why hast thou forsaken me!" (Mt 27:46 KJV), reveals the depths of his anguish. The resurrection transformed everything. With his resurrection Jesus broke the power of death, reversed the isolation of the cross and reunited with the Father.

These features of the Christian narrative contribute several things to my practical theodicy. To begin with, the cross underscores the inescapability of suffering in this world. Jesus did not avoid suffering, and neither can we. At the same time, Jesus' anguish confirms our basic intuition that suffering is wrong. There is a tragic abnormality to our current existence. We know that we are susceptible to suffering and death, but we also have the deep sense that we were not meant for them. The cross also affirms Jesus' solidarity with us in suffering. The cross reminds us that we are never alone, no matter how dark and oppressive our circumstances may be. Because Jesus endured the cross, descending to the utter depths of human anguish, nothing can happen to us that he has not in effect been through himself. Physical pain and hardship, separation from family and friends, the loss of worldly goods and reputation, the animosity of those we try to help, even spiritual isolation—Jesus knew it all. So wherever suffering takes us, we can be sure that he has been there too.

If the cross reminds us that suffering is unavoidable, the resurrection assures us that suffering will not have the last word. Jesus could not avoid the cross, but he was not imprisoned by death. The empty tomb is our assurance that suffering is temporary. From the vantage point of Christian hope, suffering will someday be a thing of the past. The time will come, the apostle Paul proclaims, when death is "swallowed up in victory" (1 Cor 15:54).

For Christian faith, cross and resurrection are inseparable, and it is important to me to see them together, particularly when it comes to suffering. Without the resurrection, the cross would be the last sad chapter in the story of a noble life. Jesus' death would be one more illustration of the grim fact that the good often die young, their dreams unfulfilled and their hopes dashed. In light of the resurrection, however, the cross is a great victory, the central act in God's response to the problem of suffering. So the resurrection transforms the cross. It turns tragedy into triumph.

At the same time, the resurrection needs the cross. Without the dark background of the crucifixion, God's power over death might appear to offer an easy escape from the rigors of this world. It could lead us to look for a detour around the difficulties of life. If God has the power to raise the dead, then surely God can insulate us from pain and sorrow; God can prevent us from ever having to suffer. But before the resurrection comes the cross. And this obliges us to recognize that God often leads us *through* perils, rather than around them. God does not promise to lift us dramatically and miraculously out of harm's way. Just as Jesus had his cross to bear, his followers have theirs as well (cf. Mt 16:24). And his promise to be with us in *our* sufferings also calls us to be with him in *his* sufferings.

Along with careful reflection and various religious influences, the experiences we accumulate over time inevitably affect a personal theodicy. My parents had a troubled marriage and eventually divorced. I learned some important things from those difficult years. For example, they made me aware of how important it was to provide a stable home for my own children. And they increased my sensitivity to the challenges facing people who come from broken homes. At the same time, however, I have never felt that on the whole it was a good thing for me to have gone through all that. Many of life's difficulties are more than made up for by the growing we do as a result, but major losses are exactly that—losses. No matter how we benefit from them, their net effect is negative. At least, that's the impression my childhood years have left me with.

When we place the religious beliefs that nurture and sustain us over the years alongside the philosophical or theological insights that careful reflection yields, and add to them the conclusions that life experiences lead us to, we will probably find that our personal, practical theodicy takes the form of a few deeply held convictions. You may find it helpful to list the ones that are central to your personal perspective on suffering. Here are the ones that form the bedrock of my own.

1. *God is Lord and God is love.* The world and everything in it owes its existence to the one being who is perfect in power and love. Numerous biblical passages support this claim, including important statements such as: "In the beginning, God created the heavens and the earth" (Gen 1:1 ESV). "The earth is the Lord's and all that is in it" (Ps 24:1). "God is love" (1 Jn 4:8). Since God is entirely good, evil cannot be a part of God's original design. Since God is love, God endowed certain creatures with personal freedom, so that they could embrace God's lordship because they chose to, not because they were somehow programmed or forced to be loyal. In doing so, God ran the risk that they would turn away from God's love rather than gratefully and joyfully returning it.

2. *Suffering is real and suffering is wrong.* As things turned out, those created in God's image betrayed God's trust in them, and the suffering that fills the world is ultimately attributable to their downfall. As a character in one of Jesus' parables says, "An enemy has done this" (Mt 13:28). The suffering of this world, of whatever sort, therefore does not express God's will for creation. To the contrary, it opposes and threatens God's purposes. Consequently, our intuitive objection to suffering, our visceral "Oh, no!" when suffering raises its ugly head, is right on the mark. It perfectly matches its negative nature.

3. *God is with us when we suffer.* It was never God's intention that we suffer, but God's love is fathomless, and God never leaves us to our fate. Consequently, we never have to suffer alone. Suffering has an isolating quality to it. Every sufferer feels that her experience is utterly unique, and no one knows exactly what she

is going through. Suffering can separate us from all that is familiar and leave us feeling alone and abandoned. We cannot help but ask, "My God, why hast thou forsaken me?" (cf. Ps 22:1 KJV). Consequently, no biblical promise is more dear to a suffering soul than those that assure us of God's abiding presence. "I will fear no evil: for thou art with me" (Ps 23:4 KJV). "I will never leave thee, nor forsake thee" (Heb 13:5 KJV). "Lo, I am with you always, even unto the end of the world" (Mt 28:20 KJV).

Verses like these—quoted here as I first heard them, in the stately cadences of the King James Version—are an antidote to the alienating effects of suffering. God is with us in the midst of our difficulties, they assure us. Sometimes God dramatically relieves human suffering; more often, God does not. But either way, we have the comfort of God's presence, whether we feel it vividly or not.

4. *Suffering never has the last word.* The fourth element in my theodicy is the conviction that suffering is never the end of the story. This conviction takes two forms. It affirms, first of all, that God can work for good in every situation. But this belief has to be carefully qualified. The most famous text on "providence," the doctrine that God works in and through events to pursue God's goals, is Romans 8:28, "We know that all things work together for good for those who love God, who are called according to his purpose." As translated this way, Paul's words do not convey the idea that everything is exactly the way God wants it to be. Nor do they mean that God somehow cancels the negatives in our lives and turns everything bad into something good. But what God does do, according to these words, is work to bring about something good, no matter how bad things may be. It is true that difficult

experiences sometimes lead to good things that more than make up for the pain. But not always. Great losses can leave scars that never completely disappear. Even so, that doesn't mean that nothing good can come of them. While in themselves they have no benefit, God can respond even to life's greatest losses in ways that bless and benefit us. In God's boundless and relentless love for us, God refuses to let our sufferings just lie there, unmitigated and unredeemed.

The conviction that suffering does not have the last word applies to the world as a whole, as well as in part. To believe in God is to believe that God's purposes account not only for the origin of the universe, but also for its destiny. It includes the confidence that God's plans for creation will eventually reach fulfillment. Suffering may oppose and interfere with God's goals, but it cannot prevent their ultimate realization. The time will come when suffering is a thing of the past, and God "will wipe away every tear from their eyes. Death will be no more; mourning and crying and pain will be no more" (Rev 21:4).

If the first two elements in this practical theodicy reflect the Christian doctrine of creation, the last two reflect the doctrine of salvation. The first two provide a fragmentary account of the origin and nature of suffering; the last two form a basis for responding to suffering resourcefully. Together, they fuel the confidence that God is Lord and love, that God still claims this world as God's own and faithfully pursues God's ultimate objectives for it.

Everyone's practical theodicy will have distinctly personal elements. To develop your own, reflect on the various sources we have mentioned—philosophical, religious and personal—and then look for the bedrock convictions that have been or are likely to be most helpful to you in facing life's challenges.

The "Grammar" of Suffering: Theirs, Mine and Yours

Finding ways to handle our own suffering resourcefully is an important part of a practical theodicy, but it is not the only part. A good practical theodicy will enable us to help others who are suffering too. And this brings us to the various ways we encounter suffering, including one that discussions of suffering often fail to notice.

The central concern of our discussion has been to identify both the distinction and the connections between two forms of suffering. When we hear about a natural disaster, a terrible accident, a vicious crime, the eruption of war or the outbreak of an epidemic somewhere, we find ourselves asking questions of an intellectual nature. Why does God allow such things? If God is all-good and all-powerful, can't God prevent them from happening, or stop them when they do, or at least limit their scope?

Things are entirely different, however, when I am the person who gets sick, when I'm the victim of a crime or when I lose someone I love. That changes the entire landscape of my life. That's when the "mountains shake in the heart of the sea," as Psalm 46 puts it. As we have seen, it is customary for people to distinguish the problem of suffering from the problem of evil—the personal experience of pain and loss from the logical difficulty of reconciling the existence of God with the presence of suffering in the world. If evil concerns things on the horizon of our lives, suffering deals with things at the center. When pain *appears* in the world, I face the problem of evil; when pain and loss *invade* my world, I face the problem of suffering.

We can also make this distinction in grammatical terms, of all things. I took Latin in high school from a teacher who demanded meticulous attention to the structure of the language. As Miss Odom explained it, there are three types of personal pronouns—first, second and third—depending on whether the person referred to is the speaker (*I, we*), the person spoken to (*you*) or someone else (*he, she, they*). To use these terms, the problem of evil pertains to "third person" suffering. It refers to the questions that occur to us when we reflect on the plight of people who are in serious difficulty, when pain and misfortune descend on *them*. In contrast, the problem of suffering involves "first person" pain and loss, when misfortune happens to *me*. It is the challenge I face when I'm the one who suffers. The two are not the same, as we have all discovered, and the ideas that seem to be helpful when I think about *their* suffering may be less than helpful, or even downright unhelpful, when I have to deal with my own.

My grandfather, for example, spent his entire adult life as a minister—a career that brought him into contact with a great deal of suffering. Over the years he preached countless funeral sermons and consoled hundreds of bereaved people. But when my grandmother died in her late sixties, he remarked that until then he never knew what it was really like to lose someone you loved. Everything is different when the suffering you face is your own.

As Miss Odom's account of pronouns suggests, however, "their suffering" and "my suffering" are not the only ways in which suffering confronts us. As it turns out, there is indeed a third form of suffering with distinctive qualities of its own. Several years ago the philosophy department of a nearby university hosted a conference devoted to the biblical book of Job. One of the participants was Eleonore Stump, an influential philosopher of religion. Professor Stump suggested that we need to read Job not only in light of first- and third-person approaches to suffering, but also in light of a second-person approach. When I heard this, I began to realize that the distinction I had always operated with was not enough. What happens when I encounter suffering that is neither my own, nor the suffering of people I don't know—that is, when it's neither first-nor third-person suffering? What happens if it's *your* suffering that confronts me? In particular, what happens when your suffering so affects me that I feel your suffering very deeply—when you and I to a certain extent suffer together? Suffering of this sort is quite different from the other two.

Eleonore Stump provides an extensive account of second-person experience and its importance to an understanding of suffering. For a second-person experience—as distinct from a first- or third-person experience—she states, it is necessary "that you interact consciously and directly with another person who is conscious and present to you as a person." She also notes that according to the recent findings of neuroscience the human brain is actually wired, so to speak, for such experiences: "The mirror neuron system seems to be a brain system designed primarily to enable second-person experience and the knowledge of persons such experience generates."[7]

So the distinction between *my* suffering and *their* suffering is helpful, but not comprehensive. Second-person suffering is important too, and responding to it poses its own particular challenges. What should I do when *you* are the one who's suffering? What should I say? What should I not say? And what role should I take? Should I think of myself as a helper, a comforter, a witness, an adviser or what? To deal with suffering resourcefully, we need to consider all the forms in which suffering confronts us. It is not enough to consider only *their* suffering and *my* suffering. A practical theodicy must take into account *your* suffering as well.

These three forms of suffering are all related, and our approach

---

[7]Stump, *Wandering in Darkness*, p. 77. In the same work, Stump develops a complex analysis of the book of Job, according to which God's response to Job (Job 38–40) constitutes a second-person account of his suffering ("nested" within other second- and third-person accounts). Its effect is to assure Job that God loves him and did not betray his trust (pp. 222, 225).

to each will inevitably reflect and affect our approach to the others. Our most vivid need is to find a way of responding resourcefully to our own suffering. But sooner or later the mere existence of suffering weighs in on us. Why should anyone suffer? we ask. Why is there so much suffering in the world and why is it so unfairly distributed? Why do some people suffer so much more than others? These questions bother some of us more than others, but eventually everyone asks them. After all, everyone has a worldview, a cosmic framework of sorts that serves as a permanent background for what we think and do. And this overall view of things inevitably affects our responses to suffering. So the approach I take to "my" suffering inevitably interacts with my overall view of suffering. People instinctively rely on certain concepts or interpretations of suffering to cope with their own experience, and they typically appeal to their favorite theories when reacting to the suffering of others. Like Job's friends, they recommend to others a worldview that appeals to them.

While we cannot escape our own suffering, it is important for us to find ways of responding appropriately to the suffering of those we are in a position to help personally. First- and second-person forms of suffering are intimately connected. *Your* response to suffering may be inspiring to me. And my openness to your suffering may be a benefit to you.

The interactions among these various forms of suffering are fluid and dynamic. As we have seen, people frequently revise their theories of suffering when they are the ones who suffer or when suffering comes to someone they love. Concrete suffering—whether it is *mine* or *yours*—can seriously alter our outlook on reality as a whole. And we may find that some of our cherished views cannot survive the pressure of experience.

FROM *My* SUFFERING TO *Your* SUFFERING

In our quest for a practical theodicy, we have explored the relation between *their* suffering and *my* suffering; now what about *your* suffering? Once again, let me use my own experience as an illustration. How might fragments like the ones I assembled from my own experience, religious convictions and serious reflection apply to the interaction between someone who is suffering and someone who hopes to provide comfort, encouragement and help? What can I do if your suffering becomes part of my own experience and I hope to help you face it resourcefully? If I were to bring the basic convictions in my practical theodicy to bear on the challenge of *your* suffering, the results might take the following form.

God is Lord and God is love. While this is the first element in my own theodicy, your own religious perspective may be different from mine, and I must respect that. As I share your experience, therefore, this may be an unspoken conviction on my part, important as it is to my own outlook. Though it sometimes happens, people in the throes of great suffering are not ordinarily interested in altering the convictions they have held over the years. And I should let you take the lead in discussing your beliefs, should you choose to do so. But whatever your religious views may be, my own views will lead me to regard you as an object of immense value in God's eyes, and that will certainly have an effect on the way I talk and act in your presence. To love the neighbor in this situation is simply to be there with you and for you, affirming your value unconditionally.

Suffering is real and suffering is wrong. Suffering people need to know, first of all, that we appreciate the reality of their experience. Suffering involves the loss of good things. Our instinctive response to suffering is "Oh, no! How could this happen to *me?*" We can affirm that bewilderment. We were not meant to suffer. At least, that's my conviction, and it may be yours as well. Then again, it may not be. As we have seen, not everyone believes that suffering is wrong. Some sufferers are sustained by the thought that everything happens for a reason, even though we may not know just what the reason is. Either way, suffering is an undeniable reality, and it needs to be acknowledged.

The longest book of the Bible, the book of Psalms, gives full expression to the depths of human woe. In fact, more than half of these ancient religious songs concern what church historian Martin Marty calls "the winter of the heart." Nevertheless, there is great comfort in these poems, because they assure suffering people that their sufferings are known to God and they matter.

Church historian Martin Marty describes losing his wife to cancer after nearly thirty years of marriage. During the months of her final hospitalization they took turns reading a Psalm at the time of each midnight medication. He read the even-numbered Psalms, she read the odd ones. "But after a particularly wretched day's bout that wracked her body and my soul," he writes, "I did not feel up to reading a particularly somber psalm, so I passed over it."

"What happened to Psalm 88?" she said. "Why did you skip it?"

"I didn't think you could take it tonight. I am not sure I could. No: I am *sure* I could not."

"Please read it for me," she said.

"All right: *I cry out in the night before thee. For my soul is full of trouble. Thou hast put me in the depths of the Pit, in the regions dark and deep.*"

"Thank you," she said, "I need that kind the most."

Marty recalls,

After that conversation we continued to speak slowly and quietly, in the bleakness of the midnight but in the warmth of each other's presence. We agreed that often the starkest scriptures were the most credible signals of God's presence and came in the worst time. When life gets down to basics, of course one wants the consoling words, the comforting sayings, the voices of hope preserved on printed pages. But they make sense only against the background . . . of the dark words.[8]

Marty's experience affirms the value of facing suffering openly. People need to know that their trials are appreciated.

In an essay in which he refers to the loss of his son, philosopher Nicholas Wolterstorff describes the struggle to "own his grief," as he put it. "The modern Western practice is to disown one's grief: to get over it, to put it behind one, to get on with life, to put it out of mind, to insure that it not become part of one's identity." (To see his point we have only to think of the facile way newscasters talk of "healing" and "closure" just hours after some terrible tragedy has occurred.) "My struggle," Wolterstorff said, "was to own [my grief], to make it part of my identity: if you want to know who I am, you must know that I am one whose son died."[9]

In a similar vein Jerry Sittser speaks of embracing the sorrow that engulfed him when he lost three members of his family in an automobile accident. To deal with the tragedy effectively, he found he could not go around his grief, he had to go through it. He had to penetrate its depths.[10]

---

[8]Martin E. Marty, *A Cry of Absence: Reflections for the Winter of the Heart* (San Francisco: HarperSanFrancisco, 1993), pp. xi-xii.
[9]Nicholas Wolterstorff, "The Grace That Shaped My Life," in *Philosophers Who Believe: The Spiritual Journeys of Eleven Leading Thinkers*, ed. Kelly James Clark (Downers Grove, IL: InterVarsity Press, 1993), pp. 273-75.
[10]Jerry Sittser, *A Grace Disguised: How the Soul Grows Through Loss* (Grand Rapids: Zondervan, 1996), p. 37.

Their experiences are reminiscent of Naomi, the central character in the biblical book of Ruth. Naomi and her husband left Bethlehem for the land of Moab with their two sons, who grew up and married Moabite women. Sadly, the men in the family all died, and Naomi returned to Bethlehem widowed and childless. In response to the excitement her return created in the town, Naomi said,

> Call me no longer Naomi,
>   call me Mara ["Bitter"],
>   for the Almighty has dealt bitterly with me.
> I went away full,
>   but the Lord has brought me back empty. (Ruth 1:20-21)

Her losses were part of her identity, and she wanted her name to reflect that. It never helps people in distress to hear that their situation isn't so bad. Suffering is important to the sufferer, and it is important to them that others acknowledge and validate their pain.

God is with us when we suffer. My presence may assure you that you do not suffer alone. God is with us in our sufferings, and that divine presence is often communicated through the presence of others. As we have seen, Christian faith places the cross—an experience of indescribable anguish—at the center of the story of Jesus. Some people believe that Christ suffered so we won't have to. But the cross represents solidarity as well as substitution. Christ not only suffers *for* us, Christ suffers *with* us.

From the Christian perspective, this is a testimony to the fact that God is with us in our suffering, that we are never alone, not even in life's darkest moments. Paul's letter to the Romans contains the ringing assurance that nothing can separate us from the love of God in Christ Jesus—not trouble, or hardship, or persecution, or famine, or nakedness, or danger, or sword. "Neither death, nor life, nor angels, nor rulers, nor things present, nor things to come, nor powers, nor height, nor depth, nor anything else in all creation"—nothing can separate us from God (Rom 8:35-39).

This could mean that God always waits for us on the other side of the ordeal, that we'll make it through no matter how bad things get. But there's another way to look at it. None of these things can separate us from God, not because God is waiting for us after they are over, but because God is with us when they happen.

Suffering never has the last word. Suffering does not have the last word for those who have confidence for the future, so an essential element in the Christian perspective on suffering is hope. For many people, hope includes the prospect of a future beyond death, a realm of existence where suffering is a thing of the past. And this is another area where it is important for us to respect the religious convictions of the one who is suffering. But Christianity provides the assurance that there is something that is stronger than anything, even death, and that is a love from which nothing can separate us.

Hope also takes form in the conviction that suffering counts for something, that it contributes to the achievement of some worthy goal. People have an instinctive desire to redeem tragedy by using it as an occasion to accomplish something good. As we have seen, families often respond to the loss of a child by doing something to benefit other children. We want our suffering and the suffering of those we love to count for something. We don't want our losses to be nothing but shreds in the fabric of our lives. So we instinctively reach for ways to mend them, learn from them, grow beyond them. Here again, Christian faith expresses and sustains this hope with the assurance that God works for good in every situation (Rom 8:28).

So, important as it is to acknowledge the reality of your suffering, it is equally important for me to reassure you that suffering does not diminish your essential value as a person. Suffering may be an inevitable part of our story, but it is not the whole story. We can be greater than our sufferings.

People transcend their sufferings in several ways. One is by courageously refusing to let suffering dominate them. This is the vital point of Viktor Frankl's well-known book *Man's Search for Meaning*. When every freedom is taken away, he insists, one freedom always remains—the freedom to choose our response. When we cannot change our situation, we are challenged to change ourselves. And of course, the greater the suffering, the greater the challenge. Frankl quotes Dostoyevsky: "There is only one thing that I dread, not to be worthy of my sufferings!"[11] No matter how desperate our situation, we can refuse to let it define us.

The message that suffering does not diminish a person's value is especially important when we remember what our society tends to regard as the basis of personal worth. We glorify the young, the healthy, the athletic. We also honor productivity or usefulness. In fact, we typically identify people with what they do. Whenever a news story mentions someone's name, it almost always gives the person's occupation as well. We ask children what they want to be when they grow up. We describe older people in terms of what they used to do. It's as if children are not yet fully human and retired persons are fully human no longer. It is no surprise then that one of the biggest worries of people who are ill or injured is the fear of losing their usefulness. When my father-in-law underwent bypass surgery for the second time, one of his postoperative complaints was the fear that he would no longer be useful. If he couldn't be productive, he felt, his life would not be worth living.

Sufferers need us to assure them—perhaps less by what we say than how we say it—that we accept and affirm them as valuable and

---

[11]Viktor E. Frankl, *Man's Search for Meaning* (New York: Washington Square, 1985), p. 87.

significant human beings. A woman I know who lost her husband to cancer told me how much it meant to him as his illness entered its final stages to have people come to the hospital just to visit, to talk about ordinary things, to share a laugh. Their companionship assured him that he was more than a patient or a victim. He was a valued friend.

My uncle suffered from Parkinson's disease and was bedridden for the last four years of his life. My aunt cared for him day and night during that entire time, with the exception of a one-hour visit each day from county caregivers. I asked her if there was anything in particular that helped him during those trying times. Yes, she said, there was one thing that meant a lot to him. His caregivers allowed him to contribute something to them. In spite of his condition, his good nature, his faith, his sense of humor came through, and they appreciated him for the person he was. In fact, not long after he died, she said, one of the caregivers made a life-changing decision because of his influence.

The prospect of entering fully into *your* suffering, of sharing the suffering of someone else, poses an enormous challenge, which is why people typically try to avoid it. The standard response is to mumble a familiar bromide and look for a comfortable exit. Seeing others suffer rattles our own sense of security, and we seldom feel that anything we do or say will really be helpful. But no call to service is more urgent than to love the neighbor in pain. And in the final analysis, no experience is more rewarding. As film critic Kenneth Turan notes in a review, "Sharing pain is the most difficult thing, but it also turns out to be the only thing that makes life bearable."[12]

---

[12]Kenneth Turan, "Dealing Openly with the Pain of Caring," *Los Angeles Times*, August 23, 2013. This is a review of *Short Term 12*, a movie that portrays the trials of providing foster care.

A FINAL WORD

We have been talking about suffering as if suffering were something we could comprehend. We certainly want to, and to some extent we can, but we have also confronted the inescapable truth that suffering never makes perfect sense. It resists logical explanation, and all the philosophy and theology in the world will never answer all the questions it brings. Whether the suffering we encounter is theirs, mine or yours, it will always pose a challenge to faith and a threat to the meaning of our lives.

But even if nothing makes perfect sense of suffering, and our attempts to fit it within a rational package never fully succeed, we can still respond to suffering resourcefully. And that is the essential message of this book. The intellectual challenges that suffering poses admit of no definitive resolution. As a philosophical exercise, no theodicy is perfectly satisfying. Nevertheless, a practical theodicy is within our reach. The mystery of suffering may never cease to challenge us, but we can live resourcefully in response to it. We can find hope and courage in the face of life's losses by bringing together fragments from the reflections and examples of others, from the assurances of religious faith and from our own experience. Suffering itself may not have meaning, but nothing can take away the meaning of our lives.

NAME AND SUBJECT INDEX

SCRIPTURE INDEX

Finding the Textbook You Need

The IVP Academic Textbook Selector
is an online tool for instantly finding the IVP books
suitable for over 250 courses across 24 disciplines.

www.ivpress.com/academic/textbookselector